My REVISION NOTES

AQA

GCSE (9–1)

CITIZENSHIP STUDIES

THIRD EDITION

Mike Mitchell

HODDER EDUCATION
AN HACHETTE UK COMPANY

Orders: please contact Hachette UK Distribution, Hely Hutchinson Centre, Milton Road, Didcot, Oxfordshire, OX11 7HH. Telephone: +44 (0)1235 827827. Email education@hachette.co.uk. Lines are open from 9 a.m. to 5 p.m., Monday to Friday. You can also order through our website: www.hoddereducation.co.uk

ISBN: 978 1 3983 7228 3

© Mike Mitchell 2023

First published in 2023 by
Hodder Education,
An Hachette UK Company
Carmelite House
50 Victoria Embankment
London EC4Y 0DZ

www.hoddereducation.co.uk

Impression number   10 9 8 7 6 5 4 3 2 1

Year   2027 2026 2025 2024 2023

Cover photo © Rawpixel.com – stock.adobe.com

Typeset by Integra Software Services Ltd, Pondicherry, India

Printed in Spain

A catalogue record for this title is available from the British Library.

Get the most from this book

Everyone has to decide their own revision strategy, but it is essential to review your work, learn it and test your understanding. These Revision Notes will help you to do that in a planned way, topic by topic. Use this book as the cornerstone of your revision and don't hesitate to write in it – personalise your notes and check your progress by ticking off each section as you revise.

Tick to track your progress

Use the revision planner on pages 4–6 to plan your revision, topic by topic. Tick each box when you have:

+ revised and understood a topic
+ tested yourself
+ practised the exam questions and gone online to check your answers.

You can also keep track of your revision by ticking off each topic heading in the book. You may find it helpful to add your own notes as you work through each topic.

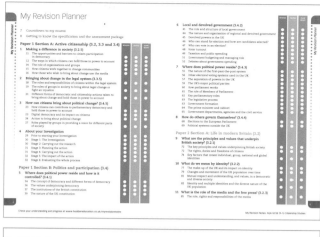

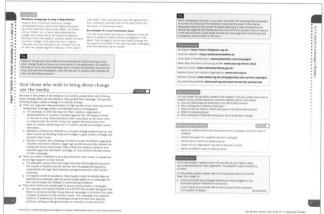

Features to help you succeed

Tips

Expert tips are given throughout the book to help you polish your exam technique in order to maximise your chances in the exam.

Now test yourself

These short, knowledge-based questions provide the first step in testing your learning. Answers are online at www.hoddereducation.co.uk/myrevisionnotesdownloads

Definitions and key terms

Essential key terms are shown in blue when they first appear and definitions are given in the Glossary on pages 129–134. You can use the Glossary to test yourself on key terms.

Key points check

Check out what you need to revise before you start answering the exam questions.

Exam practice

Practice exam questions are provided for each topic. These are written in the same style as the examination questions that you will face in the real examinations. Use them to consolidate your revision and practise your exam skills. Check your answers at www.hoddereducation.co.uk/myrevisionnotesdownloads

Useful websites

Carry out some further research and make sure you have the up-to-date information and knowledge to take into the exam.

Case studies

Case studies help to develop your understanding of a concept or issue.

Activities

These activities are designed to help you to understand the topic.

My Revision Notes: AQA GCSE (9–1) Citizenship Studies

My Revision Planner

7 Countdown to my exams

8 Getting to know the specification and the assessment package

Paper 1 Section A: Active citizenship (3.2, 3.3 and 3.4)

REVISED   TESTED   EXAM READY

1 Making a difference in society (3.2.5)
11 The opportunities and barriers to citizen participation in democracy

12 The ways in which citizens can hold those in power to account

14 The role of organisations and groups

15 How citizens work together to change communities

16 How those who wish to bring about change use the media

2 Bringing about change in the legal system (3.3.5)
18 The roles and responsibilities of citizens within the legal system

19 The roles of groups in society to bring about legal change or fight an injustice

21 Different forms of democratic and citizenship actions taken to bring about change and hold those in power to account

3 How can citizens bring about political change? (3.4.5)
23 How citizens can contribute to parliamentary democracy and hold those in power to account

23 Digital democracy and its impact on citizens

24 Action to bring about political change

27 Roles played by groups in providing a voice for different parts of society

4 About your Investigation
29 Prior to starting your Investigation

30 Stage 1: The Investigation

30 Stage 2: Carrying out the research

31 Stage 3: Planning the action

31 Stage 4: Carrying out the action

32 Stage 5: The impact of the action

32 Stage 6: Evaluating the whole process

Paper 1 Section B: Politics and participation (3.4)

5 Where does political power reside and how is it controlled? (3.4.1)
34 The concept of democracy and different forms of democracy

36 The values underpinning democracy

37 The institutions of the British constitution

39 The nature of the UK constitution

Check your understanding and progress at **www.hoddereducation.co.uk/myrevisionnotes**

6 Local and devolved government (3.4.2)

41 The role and structure of local government
44 The nature and organisation of regional and devolved government
45 Devolved powers in the UK
46 Who can stand for election and how are candidates selected?
47 Who can vote in an election?
48 Voter turnout
49 Taxation and public spending
51 Government budgeting and managing risk
52 Debates about government spending

7 Where does political power reside? (3.4.3)

55 The nature of the first-past-the-post system
56 Other electoral voting systems used in the UK
57 The separation of powers in the UK
59 The UK's major political parties
60 How parliament works
61 The role of Members of Parliament
62 Key parliamentary roles
63 The legislative process
63 Government formation
64 The prime minister and cabinet
65 Government departments, agencies and the civil service

8 How do others govern themselves? (3.4.4)

68 Elections to the European Parliament
69 Political systems outside the UK

Paper 2 Section A: Life in modern Britain (3.2)

9 What are the principles and values that underpin British society? (3.2.1)

72 The key principles and values underpinning British society
72 The rights, duties and freedoms of citizens
74 Key factors that create individual, group, national and global identities

10 What do we mean by identity? (3.2.2)

77 The make-up of the UK and its impact on identity
79 Changes and movement of the UK population over time
81 Mutual respect and understanding, and values, in a democratic and diverse society
82 Identity and multiple identities and the diverse nature of the UK population

11 What is the role of the media and the free press? (3.2.3)

85 The role, rights and responsibilities of the media

My Revision Planner

88 The right of the media to investigate and report on issues of public interest

88 The operation of press regulation and examples of where censorship is used

12 What is the UK's role in key international organisations? (3.2.4)

91 The role of the UK within international organisations

93 Brexit, the UK's membership of the EU and its impact upon the UK

95 The UK's role in solving international disputes

97 The work of non-governmental organisations

Paper 2 Section B: Rights and responsibilities (3.3)

13 What laws does a society require and why? (3.3.1)

99 The fundamental principles of law

101 How rules and laws are used to deal with injustice and discrimination

101 Rights and responsibilities in local and global situations

14 What are a citizen's rights and responsibilities within the legal system? (3.3.2)

104 The operation of the justice system

109 Rights and legal entitlements of citizens at differing ages

110 How civil law differs from criminal law

110 How the legal systems differ within the UK

15 How the law protects the citizen and deals with criminals (3.3.3)

112 How citizens' rights have changed and developed over time

113 Common law and legislation

114 The right to representation

115 The nature of criminality in the UK today

119 How we deal with those who commit crime

16 Universal human rights (3.3.4)

123 International human rights agreements and treaties

126 The role of international law in conflict situations

129 Glossary

Now test yourself and exam practice answers at www.hoddereducation.co.uk/myrevisionnotesdownloads

Countdown to my exams

6–8 weeks to go

+ Start by looking at the specification – make sure you know exactly what material you need to revise and the style of the examination. Use the revision planner on pages 4–6 to familiarise yourself with the topics.
+ Organise your notes, making sure you have covered everything on the specification. The revision planner will help you to group your notes into topics.
+ Work out a realistic revision plan that will allow you time for relaxation. Set aside days and times for all the subjects that you need to study, and stick to your timetable.
+ Set yourself sensible targets. Break your revision down into focused sessions of around 40 minutes, divided by breaks. These Revision Notes organise the basic facts into short, memorable sections to make revising easier.

REVISED

2–6 weeks to go

+ Read through the relevant sections of this book and refer to the exam tips and summaries, exam skills and key terms. Tick off the topics as you feel confident about them. Highlight those topics you find difficult and look at them again in detail.
+ Test your understanding of each topic by working through the 'Now test yourself' questions in the book. Look up the answers at **www.hoddereducation. co.uk/myrevisionnotesdownloads**
+ Make a note of any problem areas as you revise, and ask your teacher to go over these in class.
+ Look at past papers. They are one of the best ways to revise and practise your exam skills. Write or prepare planned answers to the exam practice questions provided in this book. Check your answers online at **www.hoddereducation.co.uk/ myrevisionnotesdownloads**
+ Track your progress using the revision planner and give yourself a reward when you have achieved your target.

REVISED

One week to go

+ Try to fit in at least one more timed practice of an entire past paper and seek feedback from your teacher, comparing your work closely with the mark scheme.
+ Check the revision planner to make sure you haven't missed out any topics. Brush up on any areas of difficulty by talking them over with a friend or getting help from your teacher.
+ Attend any revision classes put on by your teacher. Remember, your teacher is an expert at preparing students for examinations.

REVISED

The day before the examination

+ Flick through these Revision Notes for useful reminders, for example the Exam tips, Key points checks and key terms.
+ Check the times and places of your examinations.
+ Make sure you have everything you need – extra pens and pencils, tissues, a watch, bottled water, sweets.
+ Allow some time to relax and have an early night to ensure you are fresh and alert for the examinations.

REVISED

My exams

GCSE Citizenship Studies Paper 1

Date:...

Time: ....

Location: ....

GCSE Citizenship Studies Paper 2

Date:...

Time: ....

Location: ....

My Revision Notes: AQA GCSE (9–1) Citizenship Studies

Getting to know the specification and the assessment package

Within any GCSE course there are two distinct elements: the course content and the assessment package.

Course content: three themes

+ **Life in modern Britain** looks at the make-up and dynamics of contemporary society, what it means to be British, as well as the role of the media and the UK's role on the world stage.
+ **Rights and responsibilities** looks at the nature of laws, rights, responsibilities and the increasing globalisation of law due to treaties and agreements to which the UK abides.
+ **Politics and participation** aims to give the student, through their understanding of the political process, the knowledge and skills necessary to appreciate how to resolve issues and bring about change, and looks at how the empowered citizen is at the heart of our society.

Each of the three themes follow the same format: Concepts – Local context – National context – International context – Active citizenship. The three Active citizenship elements and the Investigation form Part A of Paper 1 and are worth 25% of the total GCSE assessment.

For more information on the citizenship skills and processes that underpin the specification, go to www.hoddereducation.co.uk/myrevisionnotesdownloads

The assessment package

Two examination papers, each 1hr 45min	% of total marks of the GCSE	Part of the specification	Sections of the specification
Paper 1 Section A	25%	Active citizenship This section of Paper 1 accesses the Active citizenship element of the themes and your own Investigation.	How can citizens make their voices heard and make a difference in society? How do citizens play a part to bring about change in the legal system? How can citizens try to bring about political change? Your Investigation: taking citizenship action
Paper 1 Section B	25%	Politics and participation	Where does political power reside in the UK and how is it controlled? What are the powers of local and devolved government and how can citizens participate? Where does political power reside: with the citizen, parliament or government? How do others govern themselves?

Check your understanding and progress at **www.hoddereducation.co.uk/myrevisionnotes**

Two examination papers, each 1hr 45min	% of total marks of the GCSE	Part of the specification	Sections of the specification
Paper 2 Section A	25%	Life in modern Britain	What are the principles and values that underpin British society? What do we mean by identity? What is the role of the media and the free press? What is the UK's role in key international organisations?
Paper 2 Section B	25%	Rights and responsibilities	What laws does a society require and why? What are a citizen's rights and responsibilities within the legal system? How has the law developed over time, and how does the law protect the citizen and deal with criminals? What are universal human rights and how do we protect them?

How are your answers assessed?

 REVISED

All the questions except 3* only assess one Assessment Objective. This enables you to more clearly understand how to answer the question.

* Paper 1 Section A: Q1.6 – 8 marks (4 AO2 + 4 AO3); Q2.3 – 6 marks (2 AO1 + 4 AO3); Q2.4 – 12 marks (4 AO2 + 8 AO3).

Assessment Objective (AO)	Weighting of the AO in the examination	Wording of the Assessment Objectives	In the examination papers
AO1	30%	Demonstrate knowledge and understanding of citizenship concepts, terms and issues	All questions worth 1 or 2 marks assess AO1
AO2	30%	Apply knowledge and understanding of citizenship concepts, terms and issues to contexts and actions	All questions worth 4 marks assess AO2
AO3	40%	Analyse and evaluate a range of evidence relating to citizenship issues, debates and actions including different viewpoints, to develop reasoned, coherent arguments and make substantiated judgements	All questions worth 8 marks assess AO3

How to answer the questions

 REVISED

A range of differing styles of question are used across the examination papers. It is helpful if you become familiar with each style.

AO1 questions often require short responses of a single word or sentence. Two-mark questions may require two distinct answers. Some questions may be in a multiple-choice style, where you must choose one correct or two correct responses.

AO2 questions are usually based upon source material, which can be a short statement or quotation, a diagram, data or a chart. These sources may be unfamiliar to you. The question asks you to apply your knowledge and understanding of the UK situation to that in the sources. You will not find answers in the sources, but sources can support the structure of your answer.

AO3 questions demand an extended response through which you can develop a case, review evidence and draw conclusions. You have several of this type of question to answer so remember to highlight the key activity you have to undertake – make a case, present an argument. Two or three valid explained points indicate better understanding than just a list of factual material.

AO3 synoptic questions. In this course you are synoptically assessed in three questions: the last 8-mark question in each of the three content themes. For synoptic questions you are expected to draw upon your understanding of citizenship issues from across differing parts of the specification and integrate them into your answer.

The structure of these questions is slightly different in that two bullet-point statements are added to provide some limited scaffolding structure for a response. The detail and structure required is no different from other AO3 8-mark questions.

The three questions that assess two AOs are based upon a case study approach, where you use a source related to Active citizenship and about your own Investigation. Remember that the questions asked have to be able to be answered by everybody, irrespective of their Active citizenship task. Therefore the questions focus upon the process – your research/planning, carrying out your task and your assessment of the work you undertook.

Check your understanding and progress at **www.hoddereducation.co.uk/myrevisionnotes**

1 Making a difference in society (3.2.5)

Chapters 1, 2 and 3 are about how citizens can take part in society and try to make a difference.

+ These three chapters comprise the concluding section of each of the three themes of the specification:
    + Life in modern Britain
    + Politics and participation
    + Rights and responsibilities. ~ the state offact of having todo something
+ Each of these three chapters follows a similar pattern but with an `a moral or legal to haveo-do something` emphasis within each on the subject content of its theme.

Assessment background

These three chapters together make up the first part of the content for Section A of Paper 1:

+ 10% of the GCSE marks are about your understanding of how people can try to make a difference
+ 15% of the total GCSE marks are about your Investigation.

The opportunities and barriers to citizen participation in democracy

Opportunities for citizen participation

+ Within a democracy like the United Kingdom, citizens have the right to participate in a variety of ways in issues that concern them. Some are formalised as a part of the political/democratic process:
    + voting or access to elected members like councillors, police and crime commissioners and Members of Parliament
    + standing for election
    + using e-democracy formats to set up online petitions on issues which may be discussed by the UK Parliament.
+ Citizens, pressure groups and interest groups can use the Judicial Review process to challenge decisions by public bodies.
+ Increasingly citizens, especially younger people, are participating in a more informal approach to bringing about change.
+ Rather than formally joining groups they participate by supporting campaigns via the internet and through the use of social media.
+ Organisations like 38 Degrees are bringing people, causes and campaigns together to exert pressure to bring about change. 38 Degrees was instrumental in getting the UK Parliament to vote down legislation to privatise the state-owned forests in the UK.

Barriers to citizen participation

+ People who do not participate give a wide range of reasons why:
    + a lack of interest or apathy
    + a belief that their participation will not make a difference
    + a lack of faith in politicians and the political process
    + a lack of information or knowledge of the skills needed to participate
    + a lack of time to participate due to their busy lives.

- Suggestions to increase voter participation include:
  - compulsory voting
  - lowering the voting age to 16
  - allowing online voting.
- It does appear that if people, and especially young people, are motivated about an issue, they will take part. For example:
  - In the referendum on Scottish Independence in 2014, 16- and 17-year-olds were allowed to vote and over 109,000 people in this age group registered to vote. Overall, the turnout was 84.6 per cent.
  - The percentage of young people voting in UK general elections has been rising over recent years (see Table 1.1).

Table 1.1 Participation of 18- to 24-year-olds in UK general elections, 2010–19

UK general election	Percentage of 18- to 24-year-olds who voted (based on post-election surveys)
2010	52
2015	38
2017	57
2019	47

The ways in which citizens can hold those in power to account

REVISED

There is a wide variety of methods citizens can use to engage with the political process, to bring their views to others' attention or to influence those in power. These can be used by individual citizens or by campaign groups such as pressure groups.

Many people now get involved in their local communities and with national or international issues through membership of or support for a group or cause. These can be voluntary groups, pressure groups, trade unions or interest groups. Many of these groups also have charitable status. By acting with others, the message of any campaign can be stronger and more effective. But as a supporter or member, you may not have so much say or control over how the campaign is run.

Petitions – collections of signatures indicating support for an agreed statement. These are used to show the strength of support for the statement. Increasingly, petitions are now completed online and are called e-petitions.

Leafleting – distributing materials that support a particular point of view, often asking for support and/or financial help.

Lobbying – a general term about making your views known to those whose opinions you wish to influence. The specific term relates to citizens approaching their MP to raise an issue. This is done in the Lobby of the House of Commons. Advocacy is a form of lobbying, where a person or a group puts forward their ideas to advocate a certain position. Often this is done verbally, but it can be in writing.

Figure 1.1 Actions to hold those in power to account

Direct action – this can take either a non-violent or a violent form. Non-violent examples include strikes, occupation of buildings and sit-ins. This can lead to protesters being arrested, for example for refusing to leave property or blocking roads. Violent direct action is criminal activity. Examples include when protesters seek to destroy property, assault others or instigate a riot. The term 'civil disobedience' also relates to direct action. This normally involves citizens disobeying rules or laws with which they disagree.

Boycotts – deciding not to purchase certain goods or services because of a particular cause.

Demonstrations – these can take many forms, from small groups to mass marches and rallies.

Media promotion – staging events and protests to attract media attention and publicity.

Use of celebrity – by attracting celebrities, causes are often able to gain media coverage and boost the number of their supporters.

Use of e-media – this format of campaigning has become increasingly important. E-media enables groups to contact their supporters quickly, give them the latest information and correct any media stories. It also enables groups to quickly contact the traditional media (newspapers and television).

Figure 1.1. *continued*

There are both advantages and disadvantages to citizen action (see Table 1.2).

Table 1.2 The advantages and disadvantages of some forms of citizen action

Forms of citizen action	Advantages	Disadvantages
Joining an interest group	Provides a focus for a limited range of objectives.	Normally interest groups are not campaigning groups. The field of interest can be very narrow.
Joining a political party	Enables a person to fully participate in the political process.	By joining you are governed by the rules of the party, so do not have total **freedom** of action.
Standing in an election	Standing for a political party means that you have a core of voters who will likely vote for you. If standing as an independent, it is more difficult to get elected, but you are able to speak and vote on issues as you wish.	Standing for a political party can limit your freedom to speak out or vote on specific issues as you have to support the party line.
Campaigning	You become fully involved with the issue and motivated to bring about a change. It can help you develop a wide range of transferrable skills.	It can move from acceptable to illegal forms of action. The issue/campaign can become a dominant factor in your life and detrimental to yourself or your ability to promote the campaign.
Advocacy	An excellent skill to develop, enabling you to present a point of view clearly to an audience.	The skill could overshadow the cause, so that your advocacy lacks sincerity. Your known expertise in advocacy skills could attract supporters rather than the cause you are promoting.

13

Table 1.2 *continued*

Forms of citizen action	Advantages	Disadvantages
Lobbying	An excellent campaigning skill to acquire. Provides you with the ability to know who to contact about an issue and how to present your case.	Organised campaign lobbying can often be less effective than individuals lobbying who are directly impacted by the issue.
Petitions	Collecting large numbers of signatures indicates the level of public support for a campaign. It is easy to organise and a low-cost campaigning tool.	As petitions are mainly carried out online, it is very easy to gather support, and consequently these petitions are increasingly disregarded. The government's **e-petition** system also undermines other types of petitioning because it is so easy to garner a large number of supporters for an e-petition.
Joining a demonstration	A way of feeling committed to a campaign and being actively involved.	If the demonstration gets out of hand, disruption and violence can occur and you can place yourself in danger of injury or arrest.
Volunteering	You can directly help a particular group of people or cause.	It does not in itself promote a change in a campaigning sense.

The role of organisations and groups

REVISED

Public services

+ Definition: state service providers at a local or national level.
+ Examples: NHS, schools, social services, libraries.
+ Role: to ensure a standard of healthcare, education and amenities are available to all citizens. A number of grants are also awarded by central and local government, for example housing associations and citizens' advice groups, for those in need.

Pressure groups

+ **Definition:** groups of people who work and campaign together on a specific issue to bring about change or maintain the current situation.
+ **Examples:** pressure groups are classified in various ways by the nature of the issue they campaign on or the methods used:
    + Single-cause groups: these pressure groups focus on a single issue, such as those opposed to the HS2 high-speed rail link.
    + Multi-cause groups: these groups campaign on a range of issues, for example, the Women's Institute, which is a campaigning body that selects a changing range of issues upon which to campaign.
    + Protective: these groups seek to protect the interests of their members, for example, the British Medical Association, which is the professional body that speaks on behalf of doctors.
    + Promotional: groups that promote their views on a particular topic, for example, Greenpeace promotes the environment.

Groups are also classified by their status:
    + Insider status: this implies that the group is able to discuss with, meet and is consulted by those it wishes to influence.
    + Outsider status: this implies that the group does not have direct access to those making decisions and is not consulted or directly involved in discussions. These groups often seek outsider status, not wishing to be a part of the 'system' of talks and negotiations.

Trade unions

+ **Definition:** organisations that represent groups of workers in terms of pay and conditions. Members from the same job sector pay to join them.
+ **Examples:** National Union of Rail, Maritime and Transport Workers (RMT). Many trade unions also work through the Trade Union Congress (TUC) to lobby government on behalf of all their members on work-related issues or public policy.
+ **Role:** Trade unions provide a voice for their members and can represent millions of workers.

Charities

+ **Definition:** organisations that are given a legal status and sometimes government taxation benefits to represent an otherwise unrepresented section of society.
+ **Examples:** NSPCC, RSPCA
+ **Role:** many charities were set up over a hundred years ago to give help to groups in society who were otherwise left unaided.

Voluntary groups

+ **Definition:** they may or may not be registered charities. They involve people working individually or collectively to provide a service to others.
+ **Examples:** helping out at a breakfast club; helping children read in the library.
+ **Role:** voluntary groups can be run locally or nationally. These groups do not directly campaign, but they promote the service or assistance they provide.

How citizens work together to change communities

REVISED

In the examination you may be asked to discuss a case study of citizens working together in their community. You should have studied two during the course. Ideally at least one example should be about your own local community. You should relate this to your own local community, as you are best placed to write about the context of where you live, but other examples of community activity are acceptable.

The following two case studies provide a template for how you might research and revise this topic.

Case study

The Grenfell Tower fire

The fire was reported at 00.54 on Wednesday 14 June 2017. Forty fire engines and 200 firefighters attended the blaze. It took nearly 24 hours to get the fire in the 24-storey block of flats under control. At least 72 people were killed and hundreds were made homeless.

As events unfolded the local community rallied round, offering help, food, accommodation and support. Since then, more formal action groups have levelled criticisms at local and **central government** about:

+ the material used for the cladding of the building
+ whether building regulations were adequate
+ the response of the emergency services.

Because of pressure from the media and groups such as Grenfell United and the Grenfell Tower Action Group, central government set up a public inquiry into the fire. The inquiry lasted five years and included more than 300 public hearings.

Official inquiry website:
www.grenfelltowerinquiry.org.uk

An example of addressing public policy and challenging injustice

This case study illustrates the power of community action groups and the media to pressure the government into action. As well as the inquiry, the government has had to invest in fire-safety measures for high-rise buildings across the country. Groups such as Grenfell United continue to put pressure on the government to hold those responsible for the tragedy to account.

Students campaign to stop a deportation

Students from a Plymouth community college campaigned to stop a family from Nigeria being sent back there after their asylum claim failed. The mother and six children, four of whom were attending the college, were being held at Yarl's Wood Immigration Removal Centre near Bedford. Students feared the family could be in danger if they were returned to Nigeria. They were told that they were to be removed from the UK after two appeals against a rejection of their asylum claim failed. They collected more than 200 signed letters from supporters, and sent them to the Home Office and Members of Parliament (MPs).

An example of a local community issue

This case study shows how a group of students concerned about the welfare of fellow students campaigned on their behalf. They managed to secure local media coverage and the support of local MPs. In this case they were challenging what they believed to be an injustice.

Tip

Research through your local media and find examples of citizens working to bring about change locally so that you can write about it in the examination. It is helpful to think about one or two recent examples and to consider the following: what was the issue, who were the campaigners, what did they wish to achieve, what methods did they use, were they successful?

How those who wish to bring about change use the media

REVISED

Because of the power of the media in our society, people who wish to bring about change often use the media to help spread their message. Groups and individuals gain media coverage in a variety of ways:

+ They can organise a demonstration or high-profile action that may receive widespread coverage online, on television and in newspapers.
    + For example, in 2003 the Stop the War Coalition organised a demonstration in London to protest against the UK being involved in the war in Iraq. Demonstrations also took place at the same time in cities across the world. It was the largest demonstration ever seen in London, attracting over 2.3 million people according to some estimates.
    + Members of Extinction Rebellion, a climate change pressure group, use direct action by blocking roads and bridges to gain media coverage and promote their cause.
    + Fathers 4 Justice, who campaign for better access for fathers regarding children involved in divorce, stage high-profile stunts often dressed as characters from comic books. They notify the media in advance and therefore gain live television coverage, so that millions became aware of their campaign.
+ They can invite a celebrity to be a figurehead for their cause, to speak and encourage support on their behalf.
    + For example, Jamie Oliver and Hugh Fearnley-Whittingstall promoted the causes of healthy schools dinners and changing fishing policy respectively through their television programmes and other media channels.
    + During the Covid-19 pandemic, Manchester United footballer Marcus Rashford successfully used his social media platform to campaign for free school meals for children in need during lockdown.
+ They work within the media itself to launch and promote a campaign.
    + For example, the World Wildlife Fund (WWF) has worked alongside Sky News to promote the Sky Ocean Rescue campaign to promote the cause of plastic pollution in the world's oceans. The campaign has inspired millions to seek action by emailing local government and signing petitions calling on the government to commit to ocean recovery.

Check your understanding and progress at **www.hoddereducation.co.uk/myrevisionnotes**

Tip

When writing about this topic in your exam remember this changing balance between the power and influence of the traditional media and the power of the internet. Newspaper sales and the number of people watching live news broadcasts are in decline (see pages 84–85). People are now more inclined to access a menu of news at a time that suits them. Social media formats also encourage direct commentary and involvement, and promotion of the story.

Useful websites

38 Degrees: **https://home.38degrees.org.uk/**

Extinction Rebellion: **https://extinctionrebellion.uk**

Jamie Oliver's Food Revolution: **www.jamieoliver.com/campaigns/**

Mhairi Black (the work of the young UK MP): **www.snp.org/mhairi_black**

National Archives: **www.nationalarchives.gov.uk/**

National Council for Voluntary Organisations: **www.ncvo.org.uk**

Women's Institute: **www.thewi.org.uk/campaigns/key-and-current-campaigns**

Sky Ocean Rescue/WWF: **www.wwf.org.uk/ocean-heroes/sky-partnership**

Key points check

Can you answer the key points related to this chapter? If you are unclear about how to respond to any of these questions, revisit the relevant topics in this chapter.

✚ How can citizens play an active part in our democratic process?

✚ Why is taking part in elections important?

✚ What barriers are there to citizens taking part in the democratic process?

✚ What are pressure groups?

✚ What methods do individuals and groups use to bring about change?

Now test yourself (AO1) TESTED ◯

1 Name the celebrity behind the free school dinners campaign during the Covid-19 lockdown.

2 Identify one reason for using the internet to campaign.

3 Define what is meant by a pressure group.

4 Explain why an organisation may wish to become a charity.

5 Name two different types of pressure group.

Exam practice

The 8-mark question relates to both AO2 and AO3 so you'll need to apply your understanding and make judgements. The question is about the actions of others.

For this sample question please refer to the case study about the Grenfell Tower fire on page 15.

1 Outline and justify two campaign methods you would suggest for the local action groups mentioned in the source.

In your response you should refer to the source and other examples of successful campaigns.

[8] (AO2/AO3)

The roles and responsibilities of citizens within the legal system

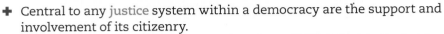

+ Central to any justice system within a democracy are the support and involvement of its citizenry.
+ If the citizens of a country had no faith in or didn't support the justice system, it would undermine the concept of living in a democracy.
+ There has been a long tradition of citizen involvement in the justice system in the various parts of the United Kingdom.
+ While one may think first about jury service, which is seen as a civic duty, there are numerous other ways citizens take part in the justice system (see Table 2.1).

Table 2.1 Ways in which citizens can take part in the justice system

Involvement with the justice system	Commentary
Jury service A jury is a group of 12 citizens randomly selected from the local electoral register.	The selected jurors are chosen to hear a case in a court located in their own area. They jointly determine the verdict of the case, making a decision based on the facts and evidence, in consultation with the judge on rules of law. Juries are normally expected to reach a unanimous verdict. Judges can allow them to reach a majority verdict with one or two jurors disagreeing with the majority.
A **witness** – someone who has seen a crime being committed	A witness to a crime is vital to the police, the **Crown Prosecution Service (CPS)** and the defence team of any person accused of an offence. By giving their version of events a witness is able to contribute to the process of justice and by their evidence prevent a case of injustice. The witness may have to appear in court and recount the statement of evidence they have already given. In some very serious cases a witness's anonymity is protected or they are placed under witness protection.
A victim of crime	It is important that a victim of a crime reports the matter to police so an investigation can be undertaken. Once a victim of crime has reported a crime to the police they have the right to be told about the progress of the case. They are also notified about any arrest/s and court cases. They should also receive information about: + victim support + the outcome of the case + any entitlement to claim for compensation + support from a family liaison police officer if required.
Magistrate – citizens from the local community who volunteer to administer justice in their local Magistrate's Court	**Magistrates** are also referred to as Justices of the Peace (JPs). Magistrates have existed for over 600 years in the UK. They do not have to have a legal background, as training is provided once they are selected. They sit as a 'bench' made up of three magistrates.

Check your understanding and progress at **www.hoddereducation.co.uk/myrevisionnotes**

Table 2.1 *continued*

Involvement with the justice system	Commentary
	They can also sit alongside a district judge.
	All criminal cases start in a Magistrates' Court.
	They can give out fines up to £5000 per offence and community orders, and can send an offender to prison for six months or twelve months for more than one crime.
	There are currently 12,651 lay magistrates, 56% of whom are women.
	When hearing a case, magistrates are supported by a professional legal adviser called the court clerk legal adviser.
Special constable – a trained volunteer who works with and supports their local police	**Special constables** come from any walk of life.
	They volunteer with their local police force for a minimum of four hours' a week.
	Once they have completed their training, they have the same powers as regular police officers and wear a similar uniform.
	Traditionally, special constables have not received payment for their work. The uniform is provided free, and expenses are paid.
	A small number of forces have a system under which special constables are given an allowance in return for specific commitments.
	In 2022, there were 9174 special constables in the UK.
Police support volunteers – people who staff police station front counters	Police support volunteers carry out general administrative tasks.
	In 2022, there were 8014 police support volunteers in the UK.
Police and crime commissioners (PCC) – elected posts, normally held by candidates who stand for a political party	These are full-time paid posts and a PCC's work includes: ✛ meeting the public to listen to their views about policing ✛ producing a police and crime plan and setting out police priorities ✛ deciding how the **budget** should be spent ✛ appointing **chief constables** and dismissing them if necessary.
Tribunal member – citizens who become members of official tribunals, which deal with specific complaints and issues	One of the best known tribunals is an employment tribunal, which deals with problems relating to work and employment contracts.
	Tribunals can advertise either for **lay members** or for those with a specialist background to serve.
	Local authorities also set up panels to deal with issues like school admission policy and these can invite citizens to become members.
Neighbourhood Watch Scheme member – people living in the same area form a committee and work with their local police force to report any local concerns	The government and local police forces encourage local residents to work together to monitor what is happening in the local community.
	Household and motor insurance companies often give discounts to people who live in Neighbourhood Watch areas.
	The police also attend Neighbourhood Watch committee meetings and report back on crime in the area.
	Together members often publish newsletters, so the community is aware of the crime, or lack of crime, in the area.

The roles of groups in society to bring about legal change or fight an injustice

REVISED

This part of the course follows the pattern established in the earlier two chapters by examining the context of how different groups can assist the citizen in relation to the content of the theme – in this case, Rights and responsibilities.

Table 2.2 shows case study examples of how various bodies can assist the citizen when fighting injustice or campaigning for legal change.

Table 2.2 Case studies of fighting injustice or campaigning for legal change

Organisation	Case study
Interest and pressure groups	Liberty is a pressure group that campaigns for civil liberties and **human rights** in the UK.
	It is an independent organisation that tries to hold the powerful to account.
	Its members have been changing the law since 1934.
	Its website shows the range of issues it is currently campaigning. One example is the Police Bill, which many groups and organisations oppose.
	Through lobbying, Liberty and others have seen some changes to the proposed legislation, but MPs have still voted for measures that Liberty and others disapprove of, such as: ✦ creating a 'buffer zone' around Parliament ✦ giving the police the power to impose noise-based restrictions on protests ✦ criminalising one-person protests ✦ giving the police the power to impose restrictions on public assemblies ✦ creating the offence of wilful obstruction of the highway ✦ giving the police powers to criminalise trespass, which threatens the way of life of Roma and Traveller communities.
	See **www.liberty-human-rights.org.uk** for more information.
Trade unions	The **Trades Union Congress (TUC)** is the body that brings together many of the UK's Trade Unions. It is a high-profile campaigning organisation.
	Trade union campaigns aim to raise awareness of issues in the workplace and put pressure on decision-makers to address these concerns.
	Typical campaigns focus on: ✦ individual safety issues ✦ defending existing rights and calling for new rights ✦ national and international days of action
	Health and safety is one of the TUC's campaigning priorities.
	It had a toilet breaks campaign, which called for the right for workers not only to have access to a toilet at work but also to have the opportunity to use it.
	For examples of the TUC's latest campaigns visit **www.tuc.org.uk/campaigns**.
Charities and voluntary groups	The NSPCC is a well-known children's charity and it also campaigns on behalf of children's rights.
	For example, the charity launched its 'Order in Court' campaign calling for 'vital changes to make our justice system fair, age appropriate, and fit for children'. The campaign had the following aims: ✦ Young people in the justice system should be treated as children rather than adults. ✦ Trained communications experts should be provided for child witnesses, to help them understand police and court proceedings. ✦ Children should be able to give evidence away from court. ✦ Specialist training should be mandatory for all judges and lawyers working on child sexual abuse cases.
	Three months after 'Order in Court' was launched, the government announced policies designed to protect vulnerable witnesses in the justice system: **https://nspcc.org.uk/what-we-do/campaigns/**
Public institutions and public services	The Parliamentary and Health Service Ombudsman investigates complaints made by members of the public about public services.
	In a recent report covering a two-month period it upheld 41% of the complaints it investigated.
	Recent investigations involved the NHS in England, and UK government departments and their agencies, such as the UK Border Force, the Driver and Vehicle Licensing Agency (DVLA) and HM Courts & Tribunals Service.
	Included in the report are cases about: ✦ a breach of cancer treatment waiting times in a hospital trust ✦ a family resorting to placing a vulnerable family member with dementia in private care following unsafe discharge from A&E on Christmas Day

Check your understanding and progress at **www.hoddereducation.co.uk/myrevisionnotes**

Table 2.2 *continued*

Organisation	Case study
	+ a woman from New Zealand wrongly losing her permanent status to reside in the UK due to poor advice from UK Visas and Immigration + a man going into debt due to incorrect benefit advice from Jobcentre Plus. See **www.ombudsman.org.uk/news-and-blog/news/ombudsmans-report-highlights-poor-complaint-handling-and-service-failures-across** for more information.

> **Tip**
>
> You do not need to remember the examples quoted above for the examination, as they are illustrative of different styles and types of campaigning. Do your own local or online research and familiarise yourself with campaigns that interest you. You should know the following about each of the campaigns you choose to focus on: why it started, what issue/s it aimed to resolve, what form it took, what effect/s – if any – it had, and to what degree it was successful in its goal/s.

Different forms of democratic and citizenship actions taken to bring about change and hold those in power to account

REVISED

This section relates to the previous two sections (see pages 18–21). Table 2.3 shows several case studies relating to human rights and the justice system.

Table 2.3 Case studies relating to human rights and the justice system

Citizen action	Case study
Joining an interest group	The websites of several major interest groups: + Amnesty International: **www.amnesty.org.uk/** + British Institute of Human Rights: **www.bihr.org.uk/about** + Humanists UK: **https://humanism.org.uk/campaigns/human-rights-and-equality/** + Justice: **https://justice.org.uk/our-work/criminal-justice-system/**
Campaigning	The Hillsborough Justice Campaign is a recent example of a successful citizen-led justice campaign. Many people were involved in the campaign, working for years to achieve justice for the victims of the Hillsborough Disaster. See **www.contrast.org/hillsborough/** for more information.
Advocacy	Professional advocates protect the interests of children and young people in the legal system. Their functions are to: + make sure a child or young person's wishes and feelings are known + attend decision-making meetings with the Local Authority or school on behalf of a child or young person + uphold a child or young person's legal rights and ensure they are fairly treated + provide impartial information to the child or young person + prepare meetings with social workers for the child or young person + assist the child or young person in making a complaint in a constructive and effective manner + negotiate with social workers and other relevant people to ask questions to relevant people and speak on the child or young person's behalf.
Lobbying	Amnesty International has used lobbying power to seek justice. + In November 2019, the Egyptian journalist Mohamed Salah was arrested and detained on unfounded charges of spreading false news and statements. + He was held without charge or trial for the peaceful exercise of his human rights for 29 months. + Supporters from around the world, backed by Amnesty International, signed petitions and sent letters to the Egyptian authorities to call for his release. + Salah was finally released in April 2022. See **www.amnesty.org.uk/resources/urgent-action-outcome-journalist-released-after-29-months-jail** for more information.

Table 2.3 *continued*

Citizen action	Case study
Petitions	A recent example of an online campaign is the case of Rosamund Adoo-Kissi-Debrah who, with the support of 177,000 people, won her fight for a fresh inquest into her daughter's death related to air pollution.
	See **www.change.org/p/grant-an-inquest-to-find-if-air-pollution-caused-my-daughter-s-death** for more information.
Joining a demonstration	In 2020, protests were held across the UK in response to the police murder of George Floyd, 46, while under arrest in the United States on 25 May 2020.
	Protests were organised by the Black Lives Matter (BLM) and Stand Up to Racism movements, and occurred in major cities across the country. Demonstrators aimed to highlight the racism minority ethnic groups face in everyday life and through interactions with police forces.
	Protests were largely peaceful, although clashes between protesters and police occurred in London, while in Bristol demonstrators toppled a statue of 17th-century slave trader Edward Colston from its pedestal before pushing it into the harbour.
Volunteering	The Law Centres Network offer volunteer apprenticeships and training places.
	Positions are open to those who are legally trained, law students and those with no legal training.
	You can work alongside qualified legal experts, helping those in need in your local community.
	For more information on current volunteer positions, visit **www.lawcentres.org.uk/lcn-s-work/volunteer-with-us**.

Useful websites

Association of Police and Crime Commissioners: **www.apccs.police.uk**

Jury Service: **www.gov.uk/jury-service/overview**

Miscarriages of Justice Organisation (MOJO): **www.miscarriagesofjustice.org/**

Neighbourhood Watch: **www.ourwatch.org.uk**

Key points check

Can you answer the key points related to this chapter? If you are unclear about how to respond to any of these questions, revisit the relevant topics in the chapter.
+ How can citizens participate in the legal system?
+ How have citizens tried to make a difference to change the law or seek legal redress?

Now test yourself (AO1)

TESTED

1 Explain the role of a jury.
2 Identify two ways the citizen can play an active part in the judicial process.
3 Define the role of a police and crime commissioner.
4 Name a UK-based human rights campaign group.
5 What is meant by the term 'advocacy'?

Exam practice

The 8-mark question relates to both AO2 and AO3 so you have to apply your understanding and make judgements. The question is about the actions of others.
1 Justify the case for maintaining the current system of lay magistrates.
   In your response you should refer to the information about magistrates on pages 17–18. [8] (AO2/AO3)

3 How can citizens bring about political change? (3.4.5)

How citizens can contribute to parliamentary democracy and hold those in power to account

In a liberal democracy:
+ the citizen is seen as being at the heart of political power
+ the citizen through their vote provides legitimacy to those who win an election.

As we live in a representative democracy, the citizen can often appear to be at arm's length from their elected representatives, therefore:
+ it is seen as a duty of a citizen in a democracy to take part in the political process to ensure that their voice is heard
+ by registering to vote and voting at local and national elections and referendums, a citizen is conferring their legitimacy on our democracy.

Citizens can become more active than just voting at election times.
+ They can join a political party or a pressure group to campaign to influence decision-makers and bring about change.
+ Citizens can lobby their representatives to ensure that they are aware of their views.
+ If a citizen feels strongly enough about an issue, they can stand for election themselves.

Digital democracy and its impact on citizens

While in the past letter writing was a powerful campaigning tool – to MPs or through charities such as Amnesty International – today the digital world is helping improve voter engagement and political participation.
+ People are increasingly turning to digital technology to engage in campaigning about political issues.
+ The government encourages digital participation through its website: https://petition.parliament.uk.
+ Once an e-petition is accepted, British citizens and UK residents can sign it. If 100,000 signatures are gained, a committee of MPs will decide whether it should be debated.
+ Another campaigning group, www.change.org, through which anyone can start a petition for free, claims that it achieves victories every day. It states that over 127 million people have been involved in its campaigns and that it has helped achieve 15,387 campaign victories in 196 countries.
+ Social media are also used as a platform for political debate.
+ Celebrities with large followings on social media use them as a campaigning tool. Facebook and Twitter are two of the most used social media formats. Manchester United player Marcus Rashford, who campaigned for free school meals during the Covid-19 lockdown, has 5.5 million followers on Twitter.

Future digital opportunities

There are many suggestions for the increased role of digital technology in our democracy:

+ Smartphones could be used to vote in elections.
+ Government ministers could hold public question time via social media.
+ Public views on issues of the day could be initiated through online referendums.

However, these changes would give more power to the individual citizen, which could ultimately undermine the power of the elected politician.

Action to bring about political change

REVISED

There are a variety of ways in which citizens can hold those in power to account for their actions. They can do this by:

+ voting
+ joining an interest group or political party
+ standing for election
+ campaigning
+ advocacy
+ lobbying
+ petitions
+ joining a demonstration
+ volunteering.

Study Table 3.1 alongside Table 2.3 in Chapter 2 (see pages 21–22). Both are applicable to the topics in this chapter. Table 3.1 adds a further dimension to this topic by considering examples of these forms of action you may wish to quote in any answer.

Joining an interest group or political party

+ An interest group is one that has a specific interest and only works towards or promotes its own interests. Interest groups seek to influence policy-makers through direct meetings or the publication of reports.
+ Individual citizens can work with others to bring about change, either locally, or by joining a national group or a group that works on a global basis.
+ If you support the ideology and policies of a political party then you can work to promote its aims and values by joining the party.
+ You may decide to campaign on the party's behalf, raise funds or stand under its banner for elected public office.
+ Standing for office can mean standing as a:
  + parish councillor, with a few hundred electors
  + district, county or unitary councillor, with many thousands of electors
  + Member of Parliament (MP), Member of the Scottish Parliament (MSP) or Assembly Member (AM), being responsible to tens of thousands of electors
  + a directly elected mayor or police and crime commissioner, being responsible to several million electors.

Other ways to hold people in power to account

On pages 21–22 you learnt about methods of citizens holding those in power to account: standing for election, campaigning, advocacy, lobbying, petitions, joining a demonstration and volunteering.

Table 3.1 provides you with examples of each type of action, which you could use to support your answers in the exam.

Table 3.1 Examples of actions to bring about political change

Form of action	Examples

Standing for election	The title 'Baby of the House' is given to the youngest elected MP. Recent examples include:
	✚ Charles Kennedy, who was elected in 1983 at the age of 23.
	  ✚ He made his maiden speech three months later during a debate regarding the younger generation.
	  ✚ Mr Kennedy went on to become the leader of the Liberal Democrats in 1999. He served as leader until 2006 and as an MP until he lost his seat at the 2015 general election.
	✚ Mhairi Black, who was elected in 2015 at the age of 20.
	  ✚ She defeated the incumbent shadow foreign secretary Douglas Alexander to take the seat of Paisley and Renfrewshire South for the Scottish National Party.
	  ✚ She made her maiden speech on 14 July 2015 during a financial statement and budget report debate.
	✚ Nadia Whittome, who was the 2019 Baby of the House after winning in Nottingham East for the Labour Party.
	  ✚ The 23-year-old pledged to donate a large part of her MP salary to the local community.

Campaigning	The UK Youth Parliament is a good example of a body that encourages campaigning by young people: ✚ Members of the Youth Parliament aged 11–18 take part in an annual debate in the **House of Commons** chamber, chaired by the **Speaker** of the House of Commons Rt. Hon Lindsey Hoyle MP. ✚ They debate five issues chosen by a ballot of young people from across the UK. ✚ They vote to decide which two issues should become the UK Youth Parliament's priority campaigns for the year ahead. For more information, visit **www.byc.org.uk/uk/uk-youth-parliament**.
Advocacy	An example of an organisation that supports advocacy is The Advocacy Project. It aims to help people who are marginalised or vulnerable because of their circumstances to make their own choices about their lives. See **www.advocacyproject.org.uk/what-we-do/** for more information.
Lobbying	✚ Greenpeace is a successful pressure and lobbying group. On its website it states that 'Decision-makers (like politicians or industry leaders) have both the resources and the responsibility to make positive change happen'. ✚ The organisation's lobbying work targets people in positions of power and pressures them to adopt environmental policies. ✚ By focusing on decision-makers, Greenpeace aims to ensure that its demands translate into 'real action that protects the environment' (**https://www.greenpeace.org.uk/take-action**).
Petitions	38 Degrees (**https://you.38degrees.org.uk**) is a campaigning website that allows you to set up your own online petition. An example of a recent campaign is the Fix the Windrush Compensation Scheme, which has attracted over 134,000 signatures. The government also has its own e-petition website at **https://petition.parliament.uk/petitions**. A recent, now closed petition – End child food poverty – no child should be going hungry – attracted 1,113,889 signatures.
Joining a demonstration	Many large-scale demonstrations centre on London. In recent years the following have been high turnout events: ✚ Stop the War (Iraq), February 2003 – 750,000 ✚ People's Vote on **Brexit**, October 2018 – 700,000 ✚ People's Vote march, March 2019 – 400,000 ✚ UK with Ukraine, March 2022 – 150,000
Volunteering	National Citizenship Service is a government-sponsored programme for 16–17-year-olds that involves an element of volunteering.

→

My Revision Notes: AQA GCSE (9–1) Citizenship Studies

Table 3.1 *continued*

Form of action	Examples
	See **www.gov.uk/government/get-involved/take-part/national-citizen-service** for more information.
	If you'd rather work overseas, the UK government has an International Citizenship Service programme for those aged 18 to 25.
	Visit **www.volunteerics.org** to learn more.

> **Tip**
>
> There are many factors to consider when discussing the different forms of action outlined in Table 3.1. For instance, when considering 'Joining a demonstration', many high-profile demonstrations involved vast numbers of people from across the UK converging on London. These demonstrations have an impact and gain media coverage, but how many actually manage to change policy? You therefore need to consider the viewpoints of those the protesters seek to influence, and why they so often ignore these types of protest.

Case study

In your exam, you will be asked questions about a case study of citizen action. If you consider the following questions, you will be prepared to answer any questions on the case study that you may be set.

Case study questions to consider

1 **Issue** – Is it clear what the campaigners/ protesters are concerned about?

2 **Aim** – What is the group trying to achieve?

3 **Target groups** – Has the group identified target group(s) it needs to influence, in order to achieve its aim(s)?

4 **Opposition** – What groups oppose the views of those who are campaigning?

5 **Methods** – What methods of campaigning do the protesters use?

6 **Role of the media** – Do the campaigners try to achieve media coverage and is this coverage helpful?

7 **Organisation** – Do the campaigners belong to formal groups and is there a structure they are all working within?

8 **Membership** – Is there a formal membership structure to the campaign, and what is the size and composition of the membership?

9 **Finance** – How do the campaigners fund their actions?

10 **Public impact** – What is the public perception of the campaign and the methods it is using?

11 **Achievement** – Did the campaign achieve its aims?

12 **Citizenship processes** – What citizenship processes were involved in this campaign?

13 **Citizenship skills** – What citizenship skills were successfully applied?

Roles played by groups in providing a voice for different parts of society

On pages 18–20 you learnt about the roles of various bodies in providing a voice for different parts of society, including public services, pressure groups, trade unions, charities and voluntary groups. Table 3.2 gives you more detailed examples of each group, which you can use to support your answers in the exam.

Table 3.2 Examples of bodies that provide a voice for different groups in society

Body	Ways in which they provide a voice for different groups in society

Public institutions	The **Equality and Human Rights Commission** is a government-funded quango, which was established by law. Parliament gave the Commission the job of challenging **discrimination** and protecting human rights across the UK:
	+ **Equality** and diversity:
	  + Promote understanding, encourage good practice, and promote equality of opportunity; assistance to victims of discrimination; and work towards the elimination of unlawful discrimination and harassment.
	+ Human rights:
	  + Promote understanding of the importance of human rights through teaching, research and public awareness and educational programmes.
	
	See **www.equalityhumanrights.com** for more information.

Public services	An ombudsman is an official who has been appointed to look into complaints about companies and public service organisations. + Ombudsmen are independent, free of charge and impartial. + They don't take sides with either the person who is complaining or the organisation being complained about. + Using an ombudsman is a way of trying to resolve a complaint without going to court. + In most cases, you must complain to the organisation first before you make a complaint to the ombudsman. A vast number of ombudsmen cover the public and private sector. The following are examples of public sector ombudsmen: + The Parliamentary and Health Service Ombudsmen investigate complaints about government departments and some other public bodies. They can also look into complaints about NHS hospitals or community health services (**www.ombudman.org.uk**). + Local government ombudsmen investigate complaints about local councils and some other local organisations (**www.lgo.org.uk**).
Pressure groups	Examples of pressure groups include: + Amnesty International + The Electoral Reform Society – an independent campaigning organisation working to champion the rights of voters and to build a better democracy (**www.electoralreform.org.uk/campaigns**) + The Royal Society for the Protection of Birds (RSPB) (**www.rspb.org.uk**) + Shelter (**www.shelter.org.uk/**) + The Worldwide Fund for Nature (WWF) (**www.wwf.org.uk**).
Trade unions	The typical activities of a trade union include: + providing assistance and services to their members + collectively bargaining for better pay and conditions for all workers + working to improve the quality of public services + political campaigning and industrial action. Nearly 7 million people in the UK belong to a trade union. Union members include nurses, school meals staff, hospital cleaners, professional footballers, shop assistants, teaching assistants, bus drivers, engineers and apprentices. UNISON is the UK's largest trade union. Its members work predominantly in public services, including education, health and local government. It has more than 1.3 million members and activists, making it one of Europe's largest unions. More than 70% of its members are women. See **www.unison.org.uk/about/what-we-do/about-trade-unions** for more information on UNISON's work.

3 How can citizens bring about political change? (3.4.5)

Table 3.2 *continued*

Body	Ways in which they provide a voice for different groups in society
Charities and voluntary groups	Citizens Advice is a charity whose work involves a large number of volunteers. ✚ It receives funding from the government among other bodies. ✚ **Citizens Advice offices** are located in most UK towns and cities. ✚ Many people turn to the charity to seek help and advice on everyday issues, such as housing, benefits entitlements, poverty, legal advice and consumer issues. ✚ The charity works with some of the most disadvantaged in society. Research shows that its clients are five times more likely to live in poverty than the average member of the UK population. ✚ Citizens Advice also provides educational services to the general public, and campaigns on social issues. Learn more at **www.citizensadvice.org.uk/**. Other voluntary groups include bodies like the St John Ambulance (**www.stjohninternational.org**) and the Royal Voluntary Service (**www.royalvoluntaryservice.org.uk**). The most popular charities in the UK are: ✚ Macmillan Cancer Support ✚ Cancer Research UK ✚ St John Ambulance ✚ Guide Dogs ✚ British Heart Foundation ✚ Marie Curie ✚ Samaritans ✚ Great Ormond Street Hospital. The wealthiest charity in the UK is the Wellcome Trust with assets of over £20bn (**https://wellcome.org**).

Useful websites

The following sites relate to other campaigns and groups you may wish to research.

Age UK: **www.ageuk.org.uk**

Break the Bag Habit: **www.breakthebaghabit.org.uk**

Equality and Human Rights Commission: **www.equalityhumanrights.com**

Greenpeace UK: **www.greenpeace.org.uk**

NCVO: **www.volunteering.org.uk/who-we-can-help**

UK government volunteer opportunities: **www.gov.uk/volunteering**

Volunteer Match: **www.volunteermatch.org**

The Women's Institute: **www.thewi.org.uk**

Key points check

Can you answer the key points related to this chapter? If you are unclear about how to respond to any of these questions, revisit the relevant topics in the chapter.

✚ How can citizens take part in the democratic process?

✚ How do pressure groups and other bodies hold those in power to account?

Now test yourself (AO1)   TESTED

1 Define what is meant by an e-petition.

2 What is the role of an ombudsman?

3 Explain one benefit of joining a trade union.

4 Name the government body responsible for dealing with issues relating to discrimination.

5 Identify which body you would complain to if you had a problem relating to the work of your local council.

Exam practice

The 8-mark question relate to both AO2 and AO3 so you have to apply your understanding and make judgements. The question is about the actions of others.

1 Examine why it is important for a body like Citizens Advice to be independent of the government.

In your response you should refer to the information about Citizens Advice in Table 3.2. [8] (AO2/AO3)

Check your understanding and progress at **www.hoddereducation.co.uk/myrevisionnotes**

4 About your Investigation

Paper 1 is divided into two sections. The first section relates to your understanding of active citizenship. The second section is about the Investigation you have undertaken.

✚ The course requires that you undertake an active citizenship Investigation. This work can be done on your own or as a group exercise.

✚ It is worth 15 per cent of the total marks for the GCSE.

✚ You are not able to take any materials relating to your Investigation into the examination.

✚ As you have chosen the title for the Investigation the questions are based upon the processes you have followed. The questions can therefore be about: why you choose your topic; how it was researched; the actions that you took; or an evaluation of the outcomes or elements of the work that you undertook.

✚ Therefore the questions on the examination paper are in an open style to accommodate the range of work students could have undertaken.

There are only four questions about your Investigation. They are worth:

✚ 2 marks – AO1
✚ 4 marks – AO2
✚ 6 marks – AO1 = 2, AO3 = 4
✚ 12 marks – AO2 = 4, AO3 = 8

The 6- and 12-mark questions are the only two questions in the examination that assess two AOs.

The 12-mark question is the highest mark question in the examination. It alone represents 7.5 per cent of the total marks for the GCSE.

To assist you with your Investigation, AQA provides a downloadable template on its website (see www.aqa.org.uk) for you to use to make notes about your Investigation and it explains the various stages you should follow.

The first thing you have to do when answering the questions about your Investigation is to briefly outline the nature of your task. This writing doesn't carry any marks, but it is important as it allows the examiner to award marks in regard to your answers in the context of your Investigation. Ensure that these couple of sentences clearly show that the Investigation is an active citizenship task and based upon the specification.

> **Tip**
>
> Remember when you undertake your Investigation to ensure that all your activities are discussed and cleared with your teacher. If your work involves tasks outside your school, ensure that you have followed all the school guidelines about contacting and working with outside bodies and groups. Ensure you keep a record of any communication with others and if working on your Investigation outside school time ensure your parents or others know where you are and how to contact you.

Prior to starting your Investigation

You have to decide whether you want to undertake this work alone or with others. Both have benefits and drawbacks and may depend upon the issue you wish to investigate.

On your own or with others? You can complete your Investigation on your own but by working with others you may achieve more and create a greater impact.

How many people should you work with? Too few and the workload is higher and there are problems if someone drops out or doesn't complete their work. Too many and the group can be difficult to coordinate and someone will need to take charge.

What skills are you looking for from the group? Some may be good at research, others may have IT skills, others may be good at working with people, others may be good at coming up with ideas.

29

Exam practice

1 Explain why you chose to work in a group or alone in regard to your Investigation. [2] (AO1)

2 Describe what citizenship skills were needed in order for you to complete your Investigation. [4] (AO2)

3 Justify the reasons for your choice of Investigation topic. [6] (AO1/AO3)

4 Examine the benefits and drawbacks of working in a group and alone when undertaking an active citizenship Investigation. [12] (AO2/AO3)

Stage 1: The Investigation
REVISED ●

Look at a copy of the current GCSE specification and consider any issues that interest you. The issues may be local, national or global or any combination of the three.

A question is where you are seeking an answer, some information or to raise a doubt about an issue or a problem that needs to be resolved.

A hypothesis is where you wish to examine and test a theory, proposition or idea. It is used as a starting point for further investigation.

Exam practice

1 Identify the stages you went through, from deciding upon the topic that interested you to finalising a question you sought to investigate. [2] (AO1)

2 Discuss the reasons for your choice of topic and question to investigate. [4] (AO2)

3 Analyse the benefits of choosing a question that either focuses upon a local issue, a national issue or a global issue. [6] (AO1/AO3)

4 Justify the argument that the question you investigated was clearly based upon the content of the specification. [12] (AO2/AO3)

Stage 2: Carrying out the research
REVISED ●

Gathering your secondary research materials Consider the sources that are available to you. Consider issues such as validity, reliability, accuracy, currency and bias.

What primary source information do you need? After reviewing your secondary evidence you may require primary source material and evidence.

Range of evidence and sources Have you ensured that you have used a range of sources and that they are up to date? Evidence that may refute your initial ideas about your question/issue should not be disregarded.

The results What were the results from your secondary and primary research? Are they clear or unclear? Is there a logical progression? Can the results be bunched around key elements of your question or issue?

The conclusions Looking at the results, what conclusions can be drawn? How do these conclusions relate to your question/issue. Do your original thoughts about the issue still stand or does the evidence take you in another direction?

Check your understanding and progress at **www.hoddereducation.co.uk/myrevisionnotes**

1 Identify some primary research that you undertook. [2] (AO1)

2 Consider the advantages of using primary as against secondary research material in relation to your Investigation. [4] (AO2)

3 Evaluate the usefulness and place in rank order of importance the evidence you gathered in relation to your issue/question. [6] (AO1/AO3)

4 Examine how the research you undertook impacted upon the wording or direction of your Investigation. [12] (AO2/AO3)

Stage 3: Planning the action

REVISED ◉

What do we mean by 'taking action'? Presenting a case to others, organising an event, representing the views of others, carrying out a consultation, writing a policy proposal or a review of a policy, setting up an action group. Which is most suited to your question or issue?

Create an Action Plan Break down the action you wish to take into a sequence of bite-size pieces and resolve who is doing what and when they have to complete their task – an Action Plan.

Getting approval Ensure that your teacher has approved your course of action. Ensure you have identified everyone you need to speak to so that any permissions can be sorted out in advance of your action.

Review your planning Ensure everybody understands what they have to do. If issues arise, have you considered other options? Have you ensured that the action relates to your question/issue and that it can achieve its aims?

1 Explain the course of action that you decided to undertake. [2] (AO1)

2 Describe the main elements of your plan in relation to your action. [4] (AO2)

3 Justify why you decided upon the specific action undertaken rather than an alternative form. [6] (AO1/AO3)

4 Justify how your form of action was a form of active citizenship. [12] (AO2/AO3)

Stage 4: Carrying out the action

REVISED ◉

Reviewing the Action Plan Is the action plan up to date? Is there a clear line of communication between group members? Is someone in charge and able to make changes if need be?

Have you set yourself targets in regard to your action so that you know you have succeeded? Have you ensured that all those outside your group who are involved in the action are aware of their role and have been contacted?

Have you considered how others view your action? Have you built into your action plan gathering data, opinions or views from others about your action? This information will be helpful when you think about evaluating your action.

My Revision Notes: AQA GCSE (9–1) Citizenship Studies

Exam practice

1 Explain what you hoped to achieve by your action. [2] (AO1)

2 Describe the targets that you set yourself in order to say your action was successful. [4] (AO2)

3 Evaluate the usefulness of the evidence/data you gathered to prove your action was successful. [6] (AO1/AO3)

4 Evaluate to what extent your aims for your action were under or over ambitious. [12] (AO2/AO3)

Tip

The exam questions may ask you to comment on your Investigation in a different way than you carried out the task. For example, you may have carried out your Investigation on your own but the Questions may ask you to reflect on the benefits or drawbacks of working with others. You may have worked in a group and you may be asked to comment upon the benefits or drawbacks of working alone. These questions are attempting to make you think about your approach to your Investigation and either the benefits or drawbacks of working alone or with others, whichever method you have actually used in your Investigation.

Stage 5: The impact of the action

REVISED

Gathering the evidence Did you remember to seek others' views about your action? Is this information in a data format that will give you evidence you can use? Has each member of the group written or spoken about their contribution and views?

Successful? To what extent was your action successful? Did it achieve the aims you set yourselves? Is there evidence to support your view about its degree of success?

Achievement To what extent did your action make a difference? To what extent did the action relate back to the points raised by your research and your question/issue?

Exam practice

1 Identify one measure you used to assess whether your action was successful. [2] (AO1)

2 Discuss to what extent your action can be considered to be successful or unsuccessful. [4] (AO2)

3 Examine what further evidence you might have gathered to assess whether your action was successful. [6] (AO1/AO3)

4 Analyse to what extent you can say that your action 'made a difference'. [12] (AO2/AO3)

Stage 6: Evaluating the whole process

REVISED

Reflect What were the succesful elements of the Investigation? What things could have been improved? What is the evidence to support your statements?i

In relation to the question/issue, what conclusions did you reach after you had taken the action? Do you feel you made a difference? If so how?

This Investigation enabled you to develop your citizenship knowledge and apply your understanding of citizenship skills, processes and methods to a real-life issue of your choice. What have you learnt and/or gained by doing this work?

Check your understanding and progress at **www.hoddereducation.co.uk/myrevisionnotes**

Exam practice

1 Explain which was the least successful part of your Investigation. [2] (AO1)

2 Consider: if you were commencing the Investigation again, which part would you change and why? [4] (AO2)

3 Justify which were the most successful elements of your Investigation. [6] (AO1/AO3)

4 Examine how your Investigation enabled you to develop a range of active citizenship skills. [12] (AO2/AO3)

Tip

In order to revise for the examination regarding your Investigation, use the sample questions in this chapter. Go back to your Investigation document and see if your notes help you answer these questions. If they do not, then when revising you should add further notes to your Investigation Profile.

The concept of democracy and different forms of democracy

REVISED ●

+ Democracy is a type of government based upon the principle that all people are equal and collectively hold power and those elected are accountable to the people.
+ The term comes from the ancient Greek words *demos*, meaning 'people', and *kratos*, meaning strength/power.

Modern usage of the term involves the following aspects, which have developed over time and are recognisable parts of the UK democratic process, as shown in Figure 5.1.

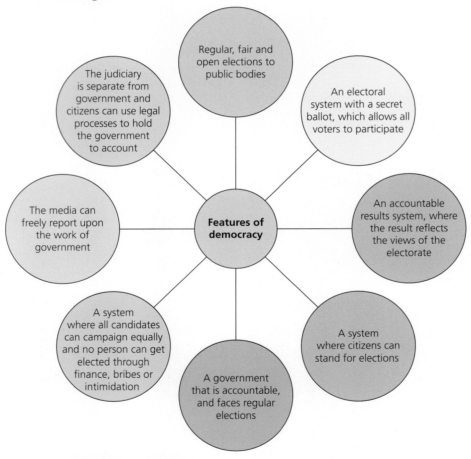

Figure 5.1 Features of democracy

Table 5.1 gives a brief explanation and examples of the various forms of democracy.

Table 5.1 Forms of democracy

Form of democracy	Examples
Liberal democracy – this concept relates to the democratic **values**.	A name given to a system of democracy through which certain freedoms of the individual are upheld and citizens are protected from excessive government power. Examples: UK, USA, EU countries
Direct democracy – this concept relates to how decisions are made within the democracy.	A system of government where all citizens take part in decision-making. A modern form of direct democracy is the use of referendums. Examples: referendums on Scottish Independence, the Good Friday Agreement in Northern Ireland, the Brexit referendum in 2016
Representative democracy – this concept relates to how decisions are made within the democracy.	A system of government where citizens are elected to represent others in an assembly. Examples: MPs or councillors

> **Tip**
>
> It is helpful, especially in longer responses about democracy, to remember that there are other systems of government that exist which are not democratic. These include dictatorship, the one-party system, absolute monarchy and theocracy.

Issues concerning democracy in the UK today

While the nature of power and the development of democracy in the UK dates from 1215 and the signing of Magna Carta, many people feel there are still changes that need to be made to improve democracy in the UK (see Table 5.2).

Table 5.2 Issues relating to democracy in the UK today

Feature of democracy	Issue	Questions to consider
Electoral systems	Different voting systems are used in different UK elections. Different voting systems produce different results. Traditionally the UK has used first-past-the-post (FPTP), which means the person who tops the poll wins.	Should **proportional representation**, where the number of seats won is based upon the percentage of votes gained, be used instead?
Voter turnout	In the UK voting is voluntary, and often for **local elections** the turnout is very low. In other countries voting is compulsory and seen as a civic duty.	In an election, should a voter be made to vote? Should we allow voting via the internet to encourage turnout?
Voting age	Currently the voting age in general elections is 18. For some elections in Scotland the voting age is 16.	At what age should someone be allowed to vote?
Power of politicians	Many countries have fixed-term parliaments, whereby the date of the next election is known. The Fixed-term Parliaments Act 2011 set a fixed term for future parliaments in the UK. However, in 2022 the Act was abolished. General elections must now be held within a 5-year period decided by the **prime minister** or a vote of 'no confidence in the government'.	Why do prime ministers prefer to control the decision about when a general election is held?
Unwritten constitution	The UK has no formal written constitution. Parliament can, if it wishes, act as it pleases.	Should a formal written constitution be introduced and, if so, what should it contain?
Independence of the **judiciary**/proactive judiciary	The **Supreme Court** and judiciary have some powers to control decisions made by politicians and parliament.	Should the Supreme Court and judiciary be given more powers?

Table 5.2 *continued*

Feature of democracy	Issue	Questions to consider
Outside interference	The European Court of Human Rights wanted the UK Parliament to consider giving people in prison the right to vote. Some countries and bodies seek to disrupt UK society through disinformation, malinformation and cyber warfare.	Should the UK be subject to decisions by outside bodies? What is the role of the UK state in protecting citizens and the state?
Devolution of power in the UK	In recent years there has been extensive devolution of power to Scotland, Wales and Northern Ireland. There has also been a devolution of powers to **directly elected mayors**.	Does this extension of democracy develop or undermine the cohesion of the UK?
Power of the **House of Lords**	The UK has one of the largest unelected parliamentary bodies in the world.	Should a body made up of hereditary peers and political appointees have the power to make and amend laws?
Use of direct democracy	In recent years there has been an increase in the use of referendums.	Should more decisions be made by the people via referendums? Should e-petitions automatically be debated in parliament?

Tip

Quote from Sir Winston Churchill, 1947:

```
Democracy is the worst form of government except all
the other forms which have been tried from time to
time.
```

When considering the way democracy operates in the UK, focus on one or two changes you would support, so you can write in depth instead of just remembering a list.

The values underpinning democracy

REVISED ●

A democratic society is underpinned by its values.

Rights

+ Rights are the legal, social and ethical entitlements that are considered the building blocks of a society.
+ All citizens within our society enjoy them equally.
+ Rights within a society structure the way government operates, the content of laws and the morality of society.
+ Rights can be limited by society when they conflict with other rights, for example, freedom of speech.
+ Rights are often grouped together and debates take place about human rights, children's rights, prisoners' rights, etc.

Responsibilities

+ Duties placed upon its citizens by a society. For example, you are expected to pay your taxes, obey the law and take part in the judicial system as a jury member if required.
+ Responsibilities are not optional and are often enshrined in law.

Freedoms

+ A power or right to speak and act or think as one wants.
+ Examples include: freedom of choice, freedom of the press, freedom of movement, freedom of expression.

Check your understanding and progress at **www.hoddereducation.co.uk/myrevisionnotes**

Equality

+ This concept relates to equal treatment for all within society.
+ Over the past 100 years there has been a vast number of laws and regulations passed in the UK to ensure equality of treatment and opportunity for all (see box).

Examples of equality legislation

Rights of women

+ Representation of the People (Equal Franchise) Act 1928
+ Equal Pay Act 1970
+ **Equality Acts** 2006 and 2010
+ Sex Discrimination Acts 1975 and 1986
+ Employment and Equality Regulations 2003 and 2006

Racial equality

+ Race Relations Acts 1965, 1968, 1976 and 2000

Rights of the child

+ The United Nations Convention on the Rights of the Child (UNCRC) came into force in 1992. Every child in the UK is entitled to over 40 specific rights.

Sexual rights

+ Sexual Offences Act 1967
+ Civil Partnership Act 2005, amended in 2019 to allow different sex couples as well as same sex couples to enter into a civil partnership.
+ Sexual Offences Act 2003
+ Gender Recognition Act 2004
+ Marriage (Same Sex Couples) Act 2013

Disability rights

+ Disability Discrimination Acts (DDA) 1995 and 2005
+ Special Educational Needs and Disability Act 2001

> **Tip**
>
> The Equality Act of 2010 brought together 116 separate pieces of legislation into one piece of legislation – many of those listed in the box. When writing about equality legislation always start with the current position, i.e. the Equality Act 2010, and draw upon past examples of legislation if required.

The institutions of the British constitution

 REVISED

Table 5.3 shows the relationship between the various elements of the British constitution.

Table 5.3 The relationship between elements of the British constitution

Constitutional element	Notes	Commentary
The power of government	Term used to describe the ability of government bodies that propose laws and carry out policy.	Not to be confused with parliament, which is the sovereign body regarding law making.
The prime minister and cabinet	The prime minister is the head of government. Normally the leader of the largest party in the House of Commons. The cabinet consists of the most senior members of the government appointed by the prime minister, who head up government departments such as health and education.	The head of state is the monarch. In some systems, like the USA, the president is head of state and head of government. Cabinet government allows for collective decision-making and responsibility. In recent years there has been some growth in the idea of prime-ministerial government.
The **sovereignty** of parliament	Only parliament can pass laws in the UK and only parliament can repeal or change them.	There can be issues when a government has large majorities and stays in power for many years.
The roles of the legislature	The legislature (the body that passes legislation – makes laws) is another name for parliament. This is done through the House of Commons or the House of Lords.	It can be questioned whether the legislature or the government is more powerful. Governments with large majorities can normally pass all their legislation easily.

Table 5.3 *continued*

Constitutional element	Notes	Commentary
	The Scottish and Welsh Parliaments and the Northern Ireland Assembly have the ability to pass laws relating to some matters in those countries.	The unelected House of Lords can often act as a check on a powerful government as its members are appointed for life and are not accountable like elected MPs.
The opposition	The title 'the official opposition' is given to the largest party not in government. It sits opposite the government in the House of Commons. The role of the opposition is to hold the government to account for its action and for members to oppose policies they disagree with.	If a government has a large majority the power of the opposition is often very limited. The 2019 general election resulted in an 80-seat Conservative majority. This enabled the government to usually pass its legislation and hold office for its full term. Governments with smaller majorities are vulnerable to losing votes in the House of Commons.

Political parties	A political party is a group of people who share a common ideology and political beliefs and wish to win elections in order to carry out their ideas.
	
	In a democratic system:
	+ the electorate has a range of political parties from which to choose from at elections
	+ political parties can either be national or regional.
		Major political parties in the UK:
		+ National:
		  + Conservative Party
		  + Labour Party
		  + Liberal Democrat Party
		  + Green Party
		+ Regional
		  + Scottish Nationalist Party
		  + Plaid Cymru (Welsh Nationals)
		  + Democratic Unionist Party (Northern Ireland)
		  + Alliance Party
		  + Sinn Fein*
		
		* Wins elections in Northern Ireland but members refuse to take their seats in the House of Commons.

The monarch	The UK has a constitutional monarchy where the monarch is head of state. The majority of the powers of the monarchy over the years have been transferred to the government. The monarch signs every new Act of Parliament into law and could refuse to do so.	Is there still a role in the twenty-first century for a hereditary monarchy within a democratic system?
Citizens	Without citizens there would be no state. Through the ballot box, citizens in the UK elect MPs who then form a government. The use of referendums enhances the power of the citizen, for example the 2016 vote to leave the EU.	In many countries the citizen makes their power felt by taking to the streets and demonstrating, which can often lead to a change in government.
The judiciary	In the UK the judiciary (the system of judges) is separate from government. It forms a part of the concept of the separation of powers. Each part is distinct and independent – the monarchy, the legislature and the judiciary. Its members are politically impartial. It is very difficult to remove a judge from office.	In some countries, like the USA, judges are either elected public officials or are known for their political beliefs.

Check your understanding and progress at **www.hoddereducation.co.uk/myrevisionnotes**

Table 5.3 *continued*

Constitutional element	Notes	Commentary
The police	In the UK there are a number of regional police forces. They prevent crime, enforce the law, arrest suspects and gather evidence. In 2012, elected posts of police and crime commissioners were established to create a sense of public accountability.	The police were never intended to be a militia, hence there are regional forces and they are unarmed. Directly elected police and crime commissioners are held accountable for their local police force. The London Met is accountable to the Mayor of London and the home secretary.
The **civil service**	People employed by government to advise government and carry out its policies. The civil service is based upon three core principles: ✚ Impartiality – serve the Crown not a specific government. They cannot be members of political parties. ✚ Anonymity – they should not be identified or associated with specific policies. ✚ Permanence – they stay in their posts when a government leaves office. They are expected to serve governments irrespective of their composition.	In recent years there has been a growth in the number of political advisers employed by the government and they often come into conflict with the work and advice offered by civil servants.

The nature of the UK constitution

REVISED ●

The UK constitution is described as being unwritten and uncodified (see Table 5.4).

Table 5.4 The advantages and disadvantages of the way the UK constitution operates

	Comment	Advantages	Disadvantages
Unwritten	There is no single written document that is called the British constitution. There are constitutional laws and conventions.	This makes changing aspects of constitutional law easy, as it is no different than any other type of law.	This gives power to the government of the day to make any changes it wishes. Other countries, like the USA, have formal written documents and specified ways to make changes that involve each state.
Uncodified	There is a range of documents containing aspects of constitutional arrangements. They are not linked or identified as being constitutional.	This enables changes to be made easily, for example lowering the voting age can be looked at in isolation from other issues such as changing parliamentary boundaries.	This enables changes to be made piecemeal that could, when taken together, undermine existing constitutional rights.

How the nature of the constitution has allowed change

Some examples:
✚ Judiciary – the Supreme Court made a ruling that the government could not close down parliament to hold an election.
✚ Devolution – increased the variation in laws and powers of decision-making within the UK.
✚ Citizens – the use of referendums has increased the power of citizens to determine policy, for example, the EU membership referendum in 2016.

> **Tip**
>
> Try to see these elements as a part of a jigsaw and consider how they relate to each other. Focus on the key concepts and from your understanding of them you can construct an argument.

Useful websites

British Library: **www.bl.uk/magna-carta**

Equality Act 2010: **www.legislation.gov.uk/ukpga/2010/15/contents**

Monarchy: **www.royal.uk**

Parliament: **www.parliament.uk**

Prime Minister's Office: **www.gov.uk/government/organisations/prime-ministers-office-10-downing-street**

UK constitution: **www.parliament.uk/globalassets/documents/commons-committees/political-and-constitutional-reform/The-UK-Constitution.pdf**

Key points check

Can you answer the key points related to this chapter? If you are unclear about how to respond to any of these questions, revisit the relevant topics in the chapter.

+ What is meant by the term 'democracy'?
+ How does direct democracy differ from representative democracy?
+ What other forms of government exist besides democracy?
+ What values underpin democracy?
+ How would you describe the UK constitution?

Now test yourself (AO1)

TESTED

1 Identify a country with a constitutional monarchy.
2 Name the political party that is currently the largest opposition party in the House of Commons.
3 What is meant by the term 'a democracy'?
4 Identify two responsibilities of citizens of the UK.
5 What is the difference between direct and representative democracy?
6 Explain what the phrase 'unwritten constitution' means.

Exam practice

Source A: the US president

The president of the USA is both the head of state and head of government. They are also commander in chief of the armed forces. A president is elected by winning the largest number of electoral college votes. This system awards so many votes based upon population to each state and the candidate that wins the popular vote in that state takes all the college votes for that state. Several states do award the college vote according to the percentage of votes each candidate receives. The constitution states that no non-born American can be president and you must be 40 years of age to stand for election as president.

1 Describe two differences between the way the US presidential system in Source A operates compared with the way a prime minister is appointed in the UK. [4] (AO2)

2 Examine the case made by those who say that the UK needs a formal written constitution to safeguard the rights of citizens. [8] (AO3)

3* Justify the arguments made in favour of the UK having judges who are not elected or political nominees.

In your answer you should consider:
+ how judges are currently appointed in the UK
+ the advantages and disadvantages of political judicial appointments. [8] (AO3)

Remember, the * means this is a synoptic question, which draws upon your knowledge and understanding from more than one theme. You can find more information on page 10.

6 Local and devolved government (3.4.2)

+ The term 'government' refers to a range of structures that operate within a state.
+ 'Government' is usually prefixed by words like central, national, devolved, regional or local. These refer to the geographical reach of the powers of these structures.

The role and structure of local government

Figure 6.1 illustrates how the UK government operates at several levels. These levels of government are often referred to as 'tiers'.

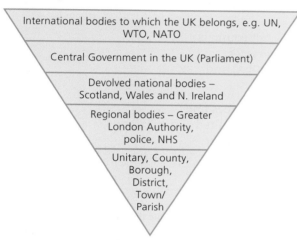

International bodies to which the UK belongs, e.g. UN, WTO, NATO

Central Government in the UK (Parliament)

Devolved national bodies – Scotland, Wales and N. Ireland

Regional bodies – Greater London Authority, police, NHS

Unitary, County, Borough, District, Town/ Parish

Figure 6.1 Tiers of government

There are two important points to remember about local government in the UK:
+ Local government has no constitutional right to exist. It can be reformed, removed or reshaped at any time by parliament.
+ Local councils are only able to carry out the functions allocated to them by central government. If they exceed their powers they are '*ultra vires*' and any spending involved can be charged to individual councillors who supported the decision.

The role of local government
+ To provide services sanctioned by central government at a local level.
+ Part of the democratic process whereby citizens can voice their opinion and stand for elected public office.
+ To provide a grassroots platform for political parties.
+ Make decisions regarding the local provision of services, for example, transport, social services, planning, etc.

The structure of local government
+ Over the years central government has changed the structure of local government, altering the functions it provides, and its boundaries.
+ New internal structures have been imposed and new elected roles have been created, like that of directly elected mayors and police and crime commissioners.

+ Different parts of the UK have slightly different local government arrangements. Local government in England and Wales, with the exception of Greater London, operates via a similar system, while Scotland and Northern Ireland have different systems of local government.

The tier system

+ For many years, local government in most places operated at several levels. These levels are known as 'tiers'.
+ The lowest tier (community/parish/town) had the fewest powers and smallest income, and the top tier covered the largest area and had the most powers and largest income.

In recent years government has encouraged the development of unitary authorities – a single council for a given area, responsible for all local services.

+ A single-tier (level) structure means there is only one local council providing all the services in a given area. These types of council originated in the cities and urban areas. This is now the preferred model of central government.
+ In July 2021, the government announced changes in North Yorkshire, Somerset and Cumbria whereby the two-tier system was to be replaced by large, all-purpose (unitary) authorities.
+ The two-tier (levels) model includes a number of smaller district councils within an area of a county council, each providing different services.
+ London has a two-tier system – the Greater London Authority (GLA) and London Boroughs.

There are also town and parish councils, but these have limited resources and powers. They are not included within the tiering system. They are consulted on planning applications and have responsibility for very local services like allotments.

Figure 6.2 illustrates the structure of local authorities in the UK.

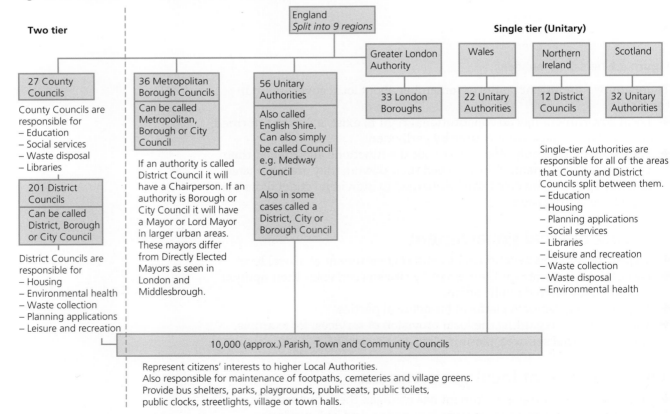

Figure 6.2 The structure of local authorities in the UK

Check your understanding and progress at **www.hoddereducation.co.uk/myrevisionnotes**

What is local government responsible for?

Table 6.1 illustrates what services the different tiers of local government are responsible for.

Table 6.1 The services provided by each type of local council

	Unitary authorities	County councils	District councils	Metropolitan districts	London Boroughs	Greater London Authority
Education	✓	✓		✓	✓	
Highways	✓	✓		✓	✓	
Transport planning	✓	✓		✓	✓	✓
Passenger transport	✓	✓				✓
Social care	✓	✓		✓	✓	
Housing	✓	✓	✓	✓	✓	
Libraries	✓	✓		✓	✓	
Leisure and recreation	✓		✓	✓	✓	
Environmental health	✓		✓	✓	✓	
Waste collection	✓		✓	✓	✓	
Waste disposal	✓	✓		✓	✓	
Planning applications	✓		✓	✓	✓	
Strategic planning	✓	✓		✓	✓	✓
Local tax collection	✓		✓	✓	✓	

Tip

Research the work of your local council. It is always helpful to be able to quote an example you are familiar with in an exam.

How councils operate

Table 6.2 describes the ways in which councils operate.

Table 6.2 How the councils operate

Operation	How they operate
Full council	The full council is made up of all elected councillors. The full council debates and decides upon policy based on reports from the various committees.
Committees	Councillors on committees monitor the council's performance and decision-making process and hold it to account for its actions.
Cabinet	Like central government, where the prime minister appoints members of the cabinet who are then responsible for departments (e.g. education), the same concept has been introduced into local government.
	The party or group that has a majority in the council appoints a leader of the council, who works with a small group of councillors they appoint – cabinet/executive members/portfolio holders – who are responsible for a service area.
Ceremonial mayors	Councils that have a leader of the council often retain the role of a ceremonial mayor. A councillor holds the post normally for one year.
Directly elected mayor	Recent governments have encouraged the introduction of directly elected mayors who are elected and then are responsible for running all local services.
	Directly elected mayors have the power to make their own senior appointments. They are held to account by elected councillors.

Activity

Council and committee meetings are open to the public and many are broadcast live. Attending or viewing a meeting will help you to understand how a council operates. Viewing online enables you to watch a range of different councils at work.

6 Local and devolved government (3.4.2)

43

My Revision Notes: AQA GCSE (9–1) Citizenship Studies

Roles and accountability of local councillors

In many ways local councillors are local versions of your MP. Local councillors:

+ represent the interests of the local community they are elected to serve
+ represent their political party on the council if they stood under a party label
+ make representations to other bodies on behalf of their community and the council
+ campaign for the best interests of the whole council area
+ hold surgeries in their local areas and deal with issues and problems raised by their constituents
+ serve on community bodies and represent the council on outside bodies
+ attend civic and community functions
+ serve on council committees
+ help decide on council policy, including the level of council tax and spending plans
+ hold the council to account for its actions.

The accountability of local councillors

Local councillors are held accountable through:

+ the ballot box, as they face their electorate when they stand for re-election
+ the local media, which reports on the work of local councillors
+ the Code of Conduct, which each council member must adhere to
+ their political party
+ an annual external audit, which all councils are subjected to
+ the publication of all financial expenses and allowances claimed by councillors.

Activity

You could arrange to speak with your local councillor to ask them about their work. You'll find a full list of councillors on your local council website.

The nature and organisation of regional and devolved government

REVISED

+ Devolution is the transfer of power from a greater to a lesser body.
+ In the UK the Westminster Parliament has agreed to establish various forms of national and regional governments, such as a National Parliament in Scotland and in Wales, and a Northern Ireland Assembly.
+ As with the local government system, these new bodies have no constitutional right to exist so could be abolished or their power and authority changed. For example, the Westminster government has imposed direct rule when power sharing has broken down in the Northern Ireland Assembly.

A timeline of devolution in the UK

+ Northern Ireland has had devolved powers since 1921 – initially a parliament, this was dissolved during 'the Troubles' (see page 96) and since then there have been periods of UK direct rule and power-sharing assemblies. In 1998 the Good Friday Agreement was followed by a referendum that re-established **devolved government** in Northern Ireland.
+ In 1998, a referendum was held and the Scottish people voted for a Scottish Parliament with the authority to have tax-varying and law-making powers.
+ Also in 1998, the Welsh people voted for an Assembly and power over some policy areas. New powers were given to Wales in 2017 and it was named as a parliament in 2019.

The current composition of the three national bodies is shown in Table 6.3. Note the strong representation of 'nationalist' parties in each body. All the elections to these bodies use a proportional voting system.

Check your understanding and progress at **www.hoddereducation.co.uk/myrevisionnotes**

Table 6.3 The composition of the three national devolved bodies in 2022

Scottish Parliament	Welsh Parliament	Northern Ireland Assembly
Government:	**Government:**	Democratic Unionist [25]
Scottish Nationalist Party [64]	Labour [30]	Sinn Fein [27]
Greens [7]	Plaid Cymru [13]	SDLP [9]
Opposition:	**Opposition:**	Ulster Unionist Party [9]
Labour [22]	Conservatives [16]	Alliance [17]
Conservative [31]	Liberal Democrat [1]	Independent Unionist [2]
Liberal Democrat [4]		Traditional Unionist Voice [1]
Other [1]		People Before Profit [1]
Presiding Officer [1] (the Speaker)		

Devolved powers in the UK

+ Devolved powers are decisions that the UK Parliament controlled in the past but which are now handed over to the devolved bodies, for example the Scottish and Welsh Parliaments being responsible for their own national health services.
+ Reserved powers are those powers still held by the UK Parliament on behalf of all parts of the UK, for example, constitutional affairs, defence and foreign policy.

Table 6.4 illustrates the powers devolved to Scotland, Wales and Northern Ireland.

Table 6.4 Powers devolved to Scotland, Wales and Northern Ireland

Powers devolved to all three nations	Additional powers devolved to Scotland	Additional powers devolved to Wales	Additional powers devolved to Northern Ireland
Health and social services	Justice and policing	Welsh language	Justice and policing
Education, training and skills	Charity law	Some income tax	Charity law
Local government	Stamp duty land tax	Stamp duty land tax	Energy
Housing	Licensing of onshore oil and gas extraction	Landfill tax	Employment law
Economic development	Some income tax	Road signs and speed limits	Social security, child support, pensions
Agriculture, forestry and fisheries	Equal opportunities in relation to public bodies in Scotland	Equal opportunities in relation to public bodies in Wales	NI Civil service
Environment and planning	Tax on carriage of passengers by air	Licensing of onshore oil and gas extraction	Equal opportunities
Transport	Abortion	Welsh Parliament and local government elections	Long-haul rates of air passenger duty
Tourism, sport, culture and heritage	Landfill tax		
Fire and rescue services	Some social security elements		
Water and flood defences	Customer advocacy and advice		
	Scottish Parliament and local government elections		

Tip

It is best to focus on one or two examples of devolved powers and be able to write about how they operate, rather than knowing a list of devolved responsibilities but without any details.

The position of England

+ While devolution has been granted to Scotland, Wales and Northern Ireland some people in England have demanded that there be an English Parliament, and others want regional bodies to be established.
+ The government has allowed English councils to combine and form regional bodies with directly elected mayors (see page 43).
+ The issue of an English Parliament is not on the political agenda, but the issue of who can vote in Westminster on laws affecting England is still debated. English MPs cannot debate or vote on NHS issues in Scotland because it is a devolved power of the Scottish Parliament, but Scottish MPs can debate and vote on the NHS in England.
+ In 2015 the Conservative government introduced new stages to the discussion of English-only legislation in an attempt to resolve the 'English votes for English laws' (EVEL) debate.
+ In 2021 the Conservative government proposed a motion that was passed in parliament to abolish the 2015 legislation.

Who can stand for election and how are candidates selected?

REVISED ○

Standing as a candidate in elections in the UK

Table 6.5 illustrates the processes for standing in both local and general elections.

Table 6.5 Processes for standing as a candidate in local and general elections in the UK

Local elections	General elections
If you want to be a candidate in a local election in the UK you must be: + at least 18 years old + a British citizen, or an eligible Commonwealth citizen. You must also meet one of the following four qualifications: + You are a registered elector for the local council area for which you wish to stand. + You have occupied as owner or tenant any land or other premises within the local council area for at least 12 months prior to handing in your election nomination papers. + Your place of work during the past 12 months is in the local council area. + You have lived in the local council area during the whole of the 12 months before the day of your election papers have to be handed in. The following people are disqualified from standing for election: + people employed by the local authority + people who hold a politically restricted post + people who are the subject of a bankruptcy restrictions order + people who have been sentenced to a term of imprisonment of three months or more, including a suspended sentence, during the past five years + people who have been disqualified under the Representation of the People Act 1983 (which covers corrupt or illegal electoral practices and offences relating to donations).	If you want to become an MP at Westminster, you must be: + at least 18 years old + either a British citizen, a citizen of the Republic of Ireland or an eligible Commonwealth citizen. There is no requirement in law for you to be a registered elector in the UK. You cannot stand in more than one **constituency** at the same UK parliamentary general election. The following people are disqualified from standing for election: + civil servants + members of police forces + members of the armed forces + government-nominated directors of commercial companies + judges + members of the legislature of any country or territory outside the Commonwealth + peers who sit in and can vote in the House of Lords + bishops of the Church of England (known as the **Lords Spiritual**) who are entitled to sit and vote in the House of Lords.

Check your understanding and progress at **www.hoddereducation.co.uk/myrevisionnotes**

Candidate selection

Each political party has its own methods of selecting candidates and this may vary depending on the type of election a person is being selected for.

The process for selecting a candidate to stand for a parliamentary election is as follows:

✚ A local party advertises in a party journal for those interested to apply.

✚ Respondents usually have to be on the list of candidates approved by the national party before they can put their names forward.

✚ A selected group of local party workers draws up a shortlist after interviewing a number of candidates to put to the local party membership. The process is usually overseen by a 'returning officer' – a trained member from another local party area who represents the national party.

✚ The potential candidates are invited to attend a meeting of party members. They address the meeting and answer questions. Through the returning officer they also send a leaflet to all party members asking for their vote.

✚ Some parties have experimented with what are called 'open primaries', where any local resident can vote at a meeting, not just party members. This is often a very expensive exercise. People vote by post or at the meeting and the returning officer is responsible for counting the votes and declaring a winner.

The local party chooses the local election candidates:

✚ Potential candidates apply and are interviewed and placed on an approved list.

✚ If a number of candidates wish to contest a seat, local party members meet and vote to select them.

Who can vote in an election?

Local elections

To vote in a local council election you must be on the electoral register and also one of the following:

✚ be of voting age – 16 in Scotland and Wales, 18 in England – on the day of the election

✚ be a British citizen, a qualifying Commonwealth citizen, or a citizen of a country that has an agreement with the UK, for example, Spain and Portugal.

General elections

To vote in a UK general election a person must be registered to vote and also:

✚ aged 18 or over

✚ be a British citizen, a qualifying Commonwealth citizen or a citizen of the Republic of Ireland

The following people cannot vote in a UK general election:

✚ members of the House of Lords (although they can vote in elections to local authorities, devolved legislatures and the European Parliament)

✚ anyone other than British, Irish and qualifying Commonwealth citizens

✚ convicted persons in prison (though remand prisoners – prisoners awaiting trial – can vote if they are on the electoral register)

✚ anyone found guilty within the previous five years of corrupt or illegal practices in connection with an election

✚ anyone who has been detained under certain sections of the Mental Health Act 1983.

Registering to vote

✚ In England and Northern Ireland you can register to vote when you are 16. However, you can only vote when you are 18.

47

+ In Scotland and Wales you can register to vote when you are 15. You can vote in local and Scottish/Welsh Parliament elections when you are 16 and UK parliamentary elections when you are 18.

The debate about the voting age

During the twentieth century, there were many debates about who could vote and at what age.

+ Women were first given the vote in general elections in 1918, but they had to be 30 years old. Men could vote at 21.
+ In 1928, all women over 21 were allowed to vote.
+ In 1970, the voting age was lowered to 18.
+ In the referendum on Scottish independence the voting age was 16.
+ In Scotland and Wales the voting age in local and devolved elections is 16.

Many people now argue that the voting age should be lowered to 16 for all parts of the UK and for all elections, and many of the major political parties support this.

> **Tip**
>
> Remember, when writing about issues such as lowering the voting age there is no right or wrong answer. All you need do is justify your point of view with evidence.

Voter turnout

REVISED

Voter turnout relates to the number of people who vote as a percentage of the number of people who could vote.

+ For a number of years, politicians have been concerned about the voter registration and turnout at various UK elections. This was one of the factors behind introducing Citizenship as a National Curriculum subject in schools.
+ Many argue that this lack of turnout is due to **voter apathy** – people not being interested in politics or becoming disillusioned with the political process.

Table 6.6 illustrates the turnout in different types of UK elections between 2012 and 2019.

Table 6.6 Turnout in different UK elections between 2012 and 2019

Year	Type of election	Percentage turnout (%)
2019	General election	67.3
2019	EU parliamentary	36.9
2018	Local election (average)	35.0
2017	Northern Ireland Assembly	64.0
2016	EU referendum	72.0
2016	Scottish Parliament	55.6
2016	Welsh Assembly	45.5
2016	Mayor of London	45.3
2014	Scottish Independence referendum	84.6
2012	Police and crime commissioners	15.0

Figure 6.3 indicates voting behaviour by age range in the 2019 general election. Several key points emerge from this data:

+ Only 47 per cent of voters aged 18 to 24 voted, a decrease of 7 per cent compared to the 2017 general election. A total of 74 per cent of over 65-year-olds voted in 2019.

- The older the person, the more likely they were to vote Conservative.
- The younger the person, the more likely they were to vote Labour.

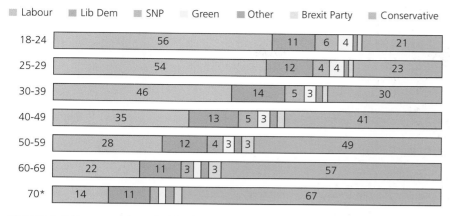

Figure 6.3 How people voted in the 2019 general election by age

Source: https://yougov.co.uk/topics/politics/articles-reports/2019/12/17/how-britain-voted-2019-general-election

Suggestions for improving voter turnout

- The Electoral Commission is the government body responsible for the running of elections.
- The Commission has published reports looking at changes that might encourage more people to vote. A number of methods have been tried out in some local elections. These include:
  - allowing weekend voting
  - changing polling hours
  - opening polling stations in different locations
  - encouraging postal and early voting.
- It was found that when 100 per cent postal vote local elections took place the turnout increased.
- Currently no changes have been made beyond making it easier to go on the electoral register and obtain a postal vote.
- Others have suggested online voting or telephone voting. These are all system changes to get people more interested and involved in politics. But is it politics and the way we do politics that have to change? Suggestions include:
  - changing the voting system to a proportional system so voters feel their vote counts – this is already in use in some elections in Scotland, Wales and Northern Ireland
  - making more use of local referendums
  - ensuring that more e-petitions are discussed and acted upon by parliament
  - introducing compulsory voting as employed in other countries, such as Australia.

> **Tip**
>
> When writing about elections or voting remember to use contemporary evidence, not material from 50 or 100 years ago.

Taxation and public spending

REVISED ●

Figures 6.4 and 6.5 indicate the government planned spending and income for 2021/22. These figures are updated annually when the chancellor of the exchequer introduces the annual Budget. The tax year starts on 6 April each year and Budget announcements are normally made in March.

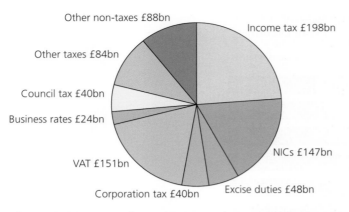

Figure 6.4 Sources of UK government income, 2021/22

Source: adapted from Office for Budget Responsibility and HM Treasury calculations

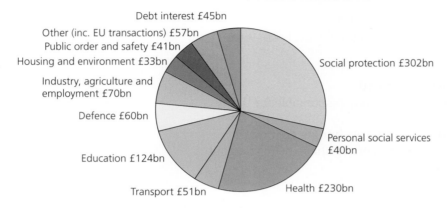

Figure 6.5 UK government spending, 2021/22

Source: adapted from Office for Budget Responsibility and HM Treasury calculations

Table 6.7 illustrates central government income and spending based on the data shown in Figures 6.4 and 6.5.

Table 6.7 Central government income and spending – notes on Figures 6.4 and 6.5

Government income	Government spending
The main sources of government income are: + income tax paid by everyone earning or having an investment or savings income above a set annual level + National Insurance contributions (NICs) paid by everyone aged below 65, in employment, earning above a set level + value-added tax (VAT) paid on a large range of goods and services + corporation tax paid by companies on their profits + business rates paid by businesses based on the value of their properties + excise duties – taxes on things like alcohol and cigarettes.	Once a government has an agreed spending programme, it must decide how to raise the money to pay for the services it wishes to provide. It can do this through taxation or by increasing its debts. + Welfare related spending, personal social services, health, education and social protection account for a very large part of government spending. + Debt interest relates to the interest the government pays on the national debt that has accumulated over several hundred years. + Government debt is the money governments borrow to finance long-term projects. The UK debt has built up over hundreds of years and includes money borrowed during wartime. It is both a source of income and debt. We pay annual interest on the debt and pay off some of the debt from time to time.

Local government income and spending

+ Council tax is the annual tax levied by local councils on properties in their local area.
+ The rest of the local government's income comes from charges they make for their services, for example, parking, leisure services, planning applications, etc.
+ Local government spending relates to the services shown on page 43.

National and local government income

+ Local government income and spending is ultimately controlled by central government.
+ National government has regulations in place to force local councils to hold a local referendum if they wish to raise council tax beyond a percentage set by central government.
+ Central government also sets other income streams for local government, the amount of business rates received and funds relating to house building in the local area. Grants are also available but linked to central government objectives.

> **Tip**
>
> When discussing figures like those that form the Budget you don't need to know the figure to the nearest million – you just need to show you understand the scale of the finances involved. Instead use, for example, 'more than £400 million' or 'several billions'.

Government budgeting and managing risk

 REVISED

Planned budgetary decisions

+ Once in power a government needs to establish a Budget.
+ The budgetary promises a government makes are based on the political philosophy of the party, for example, whether it is in favour of higher or lower government spending and what was in its election manifesto.
+ Some budgetary decisions are short term and deal with an immediate crisis, like the Covid-19 pandemic, but others, such as dealing with an ageing population, are long term.
+ Governments have three options if they wish to increase government spending:
    + increase taxation to generate more government income
    + borrow additional money thereby increasing the government debt
    + make assumptions about economic growth which will lead to existing taxes raising more income.

Unforeseen budgetary decisions – managing risk

Many budgetary decisions occur once a government is in office. They are not planned and require almost instant decisions. For example:

+ The Covid-19 pandemic: huge amounts of money were needed to support the NHS in caring for patients and introducing a national vaccination campaign. Businesses required financial assistance from the government in order to continue operating.
+ The war in Ukraine: the displacement of millions of people and the rising food and energy insecurity led to an increase in the cost of living in the UK with higher energy costs and prices of goods and services.

If the economy is growing it is easier for the state to spend more money and it can actually take a lower percentage of the nation's gross domestic product (GDP) in taxation at the same time.

Problems arise when there is a crisis or economic growth stops or goes into reverse. A government is then trapped by greater demands for its services due to increased unemployment and lower spending in the economy cutting its tax revenues. It can also be committed to maintaining the existing levels of provision, which may have become more generous during the years of growth.

Impacts of government budgeting on citizens

✛ Governments use their economic policy decisions and budgeting proposals both for economic and political purposes. All economic decisions made by governments impact on citizens' lives; whether that is increasing or cutting public spending, or raising or lowering levels of taxation.

✛ Recently there has been a political debate about raising pensions and benefits in line with inflation or the lower rate of wage increases. Using wage inflation means that those on benefits – often the poorest in society – will see their living standards fall. Politically, those aged over 65 are those who are more likely to vote.

✛ During the winter fuel crisis of 2022, the government gave every household £400, and pensioners and those on benefits received additional payments. Some households that received the £400 may have been able to afford this increase anyway, but the government were reacting to an emergency situation due to the combined impact of a cost-of-living crisis.

If you were in government, what would have done about the benefits and pensions increase? Would you have delayed the energy payments so that you could target the money better? Remember that at the same time the government are looking to make budget savings.

Debates about government spending

REVISED

Table 6.8 shows a range of differing viewpoints regarding government provision for welfare, health, the elderly and education.

> **Tip**
>
> You need to consider which viewpoint you support and whether you can provide sufficient evidence to support your point of view.

Table 6.8 Government provision for welfare, health, the elderly and education

Service provision	Case study	Differing viewpoints
Welfare benefits	The overall budget requirement for welfare benefits increases year on year.	The state should provide a basic income to allow those in need to live a normal life.
		By cutting back on welfare payments claimants are encouraged to go out and look for work.
		By freezing or cutting benefits a government appears indifferent to the needs of the poorest.
Health	The NHS always claims it needs increased funding. This is especially so now that social care is a part of the NHS budget. Every government spends more on health service provision but it never appears sufficient and there are always service-related issues.	The state should involve a range of providers (from the private and voluntary sector) of NHS services so they promote competition and enable the service to become more efficient.
		The NHS should be funded from general taxation and it should be given additional money every year to maintain and improve services. It should remain free of charge at the point of delivery for everyone.
		People should be encouraged to take out private medical insurance.
		NHS funding should be taken out of politics through its funding being independently decided.

52

Table 6.8 *continued*

Service provision	Case study	Differing viewpoints
Elderly	State pensions are currently decided through a triple lock provision, whereby pensioners receive the higher figure of wage **inflation**, CPI (Consumer Price Index) or 2.5%. In 2022 the triple lock was suspended. Pensioners were awarded 3.1% while wage inflation was 7%.	The triple lock provides some security for the poorest and most vulnerable in society. 2.5% is the least they deserve each year. In recent years the triple lock has protected pensioners' income. It is now time to help others in society.
Education	Each school in the country is currently funded on a formula that has not been changed for many years. The government has proposed changing the formula to treat schools more equally. Some schools would see an increase in funding while others would lose out.	The system must be made fairer but within the existing Budget allocation, so there will be winners and losers. We need to invest more money in our schools to improve pupil outcomes in order to provide the skilled workforce for tomorrow. Funding isn't the issue. There needs to be more competition between schools to raise standards.

Useful websites

The Electoral Commission: **www.electoralcommission.org.uk**

Greater London Authority: **www.london.gov.uk**

Local Government Association: **www.local.gov.uk**

Northern Ireland Assembly: **www.niassembly.gov.uk**

Scottish Parliament: **www.parliament.scot/**

UK Budget: **www.gov.uk/government/publications/budget-2021-documents/budget-2021-html**

UK government: **www.gov.uk**

UK Parliament: **www.parliament.uk**

Welsh Parliament: **https://senedd.wales**

Key points check

Can you answer the key points related to this chapter? If you are unclear about how to respond to any of these questions, revisit the relevant topics in the chapter.
+ What does local government do and how is it organised in the UK?
+ How does my local council make decisions?
+ What is devolution and how does it work in the UK?
+ How can I become a candidate in an election?
+ Why is voter apathy an issue?
+ How does the government raise and spend its income?

Now test yourself (AO1)   TESTED ○

1 Name a major source of central government income.
2 Identify one source of local authority income.
3 Explain what is meant by the term 'devolution'.
4 Identify which parts of the UK have their own national parliament.
5 Explain one role of an elected local councillor.
6 Name the body that oversees the running of elections and referendums in the UK.

My Revision Notes: AQA GCSE (9–1) Citizenship Studies

Exam practice

1 Using Table 6.6 on page 48, discuss why some elections have a higher
turnout than others. [4] (AO2)

2 Justify a case for raising taxation in order to spend more money
on the NHS. [8] (AO3)

3* Many people say their vote doesn't count or is a wasted vote as the
party they vote for never wins the seat. Justify a case that says changing
the voting system for electing MPs would increase voter turnout and
decrease voter apathy.

In your answer you should consider:
+ the range of voting systems available
+ how to end voter apathy and increase voter turnout. [8] (AO3)

Remember, the * means this is a synoptic question, which draws upon your
knowledge and understanding from more than one theme. You can find more
information on page 10.

Check your understanding and progress at **www.hoddereducation.co.uk/myrevisionnotes**

7 Where does political power reside? (3.4.3)

The nature of the first-past-the-post system

REVISED

+ The UK is a representative democracy.
+ Approximately every five years the electorate votes and elects a new parliament.
+ Parliament comprises 650 MPs.

A constituency

+ Every MP represents a constituency.
+ A constituency is a geographical area made up of between 69,724 and 77,062 electors (voters).
+ In 2023 new boundaries come into force where each **constituency** will have a similar electorate.
+ Each constituency elects one MP using the first-past-the-post (FPTP) electoral system.

Date of the election

+ By tradition, general elections are held on Thursdays.
+ In 2022 the Fixed-term Parliaments Act 2012 was abolished so that now a prime minister can decide the date of the general election. It must be held within five years of the last election.
+ If a government loses a vote of no confidence in the House of Commons an election must take place.

How does the FPTP system work?

+ Each voter who is registered on the electoral register votes by either:
    + going to a polling station
    + voting by post
    + having a proxy vote whereby someone votes on their behalf.
+ At the polling station each voter is given a ballot paper. They place an X against the candidate of their choice and then place their ballot paper in a ballot box.
+ When the votes are counted, the candidate with the most votes is elected.

A by-election

+ When an MP dies, resigns or there is a recall petition* a by-election is called. The seat is not left vacant until the next general election but an election is held in that seat to elect a new MP.

Recall petitions

* If 10% of an MP's electors sign a recall position a by-election is called. A recall petition relates to when an MP has any one of the following:
+ a **custodial** prison sentence (including a suspended sentence)
+ suspension from the House of at least ten sitting days or 14 calendar days, following a report by the Committee on Standards
+ a conviction for providing false or misleading expenses claims.

Table 7.1 shows the results of the 2019 general election.

Table 7.1 The 2019 general election results

Party	MPs elected	Party vote (millions)	Percentage of national vote
Conservative Party	365	14.0	43.6
Labour Party	202	10.3	32.2
Liberal Democrat Party	11	3.7	11.5
Green Party	1	0.86	2.7
Brexit Party	–	0.64	2.0
Scottish National Party*	48	1.2	3.9
Democratic Unionist Party*	8	0.24	0.8
Sinn Féin*	7	0.18	0.6
Alliance*	1	0.13	0.4
Social and Democratic Labour Party*	2	0.11	0.1
Plaid Cymru*	4	0.15	0.5
Speaker	1	–	–

* Parties that only contest constituencies in a part of the UK: Scotland, Wales or Northern Ireland.

> **Tip**
>
> Always ensure that you study the latest general elections results and that you are able to quote the outcome in any response.

Other electoral voting systems used in the UK

REVISED

As well as FPTP, a range of other systems are used for different elections in the UK (see Table 7.2). Voting systems fall into two types:

+ Proportional systems: the number of votes given to a party at an election is reflected in the number of people elected. For example, if the House of Commons had 600 members and the Green Party won 10 per cent of the vote, it would expect to have 60 MPs.
+ Non-proportional systems like FPTP: in an FPTP system there is no link between the national vote for a party and the number of MPs elected. MPs are elected by gaining the most votes in their individual constituencies. Another example of a non-proportional voting system involves two rounds of voting where only the top two candidates go through to the second round (French presidential system).

Table 7.2 Voting systems used in the UK

Voting system and examples	Description	Advantages	Disadvantages
First-past-the-post (FPTP) UK Parliament	The candidate with most votes wins. A non-proportional system. A referendum was held in May 2012 to change the way the UK elects MPs to the alternative vote system. The proposal was rejected.	The system is simple to use. The outcome is known quickly.	People can be elected on a minority of the vote. Governments are elected on a minority of the vote. Smaller parties are under-represented.
Local authority elections in England and Wales	Councils can choose to call an election every three years, or use a thirds system whereby one third of the members are elected each year. County councillors are elected every four years.		

Check your understanding and progress at **www.hoddereducation.co.uk/myrevisionnotes**

Table 7.2 continued

Voting system and examples	Description	Advantages	Disadvantages
Single transferrable vote (STV) Northern Ireland Assembly Northern Ireland local councils, Scottish local councils	Proportional system where the electors place candidates in number order. Each candidate must achieve a quota of votes to win. Votes above the quota are redistributed to the voters' lower choices.	Every vote does help elect someone. The result closely matches the votes cast for each party.	This system often leads to many parties electing candidates. **Coalition governments** are more likely. Results can take time to count.
Supplementary vote (SV)* Directly elected mayors Police and crime commissioners	Voters have a first and second choice candidate. The winner must receive over 50% of the votes. Lowest scoring candidates are removed and their second votes redistributed.	Ensures that the winner has over 50% of the votes cast.	Often the winner relies on others' second choices.
Additional member system (AMS) Scottish Parliament Welsh Parliament Greater London Authority	Voters have two votes, one for a candidate and the second for a party list. The first votes operate as an FPTP system and the second acts as a top-up vote to ensure that the overall vote is proportional when additional members are elected from the party list.	Ensures that the wishes of the voters are more closely aligned to the outcome.	Ends up with two types of elected member – one directly elected and another from a list.

* In 2022 the government proposed altering the voting system for police and crime commissioners and directly elected mayors to the FPTP system.

> **Tip**
>
> Start revising this section by being clear about the two types of voting systems: proportional and non-proportional. Revise how one example of each works and its advantages and disadvantages.

The separation of powers in the UK

REVISED ⬤

This section of the course relates to the different elements and ideas that make up how parliament works.

The executive, legislature, judiciary and the monarchy

Table 7.3 illustrates the separation of powers in the UK.

Table 7.3 The separation of powers in the UK

The executive	The legislature
Branch of government made up of the prime minister and other ministers, senior civil servants and policy advisors. It drafts and then, in the case of the civil service, implements the policy after it has been agreed by the legislature.	The legislature is the body that makes the laws. In the UK it is parliament sitting in Westminster, made up of the House of Commons and the House of Lords.

My Revision Notes: AQA GCSE (9–1) Citizenship Studies

Table 7.3 *continued*

The judiciary	The monarchy
Comprises the judges involved in the legal process.	Monarchy is a traditional form of government whereby power is passed down through the family line.
Decisions made by government ministers and parliament can be challenged in a court.	The UK is a constitutional monarchy.
Often legislation is not clearly worded, so judges have to make a determination regarding its meaning.	Most of the powers that belonged to the monarch have been transferred to the government.
While the judiciary is supposed to be separate and independent, it can become 'political' by the decisions it makes.	All citizens of the UK are subjects of the monarch.
If the government does not like the interpretation of a law by judges it can draft new laws or regulations to achieve what was originally intended.	The role of the monarchy today is largely ceremonial.

Figure 7.1 illustrates the nature of the bicameral Westminster Parliament. It is a system followed in many other countries, for example, the Congress (parliament) of the USA is made up of the House of Representatives and the Senate.

BICAMERAL PARLIAMENT
In the UK, parliament is made up of two parts (chambers): the House of Commons and the House of Lords.

The monarch
- Appoints a prime minister after each general election.
- Formally opens parliament and reads the King's Speech.
- Formally dissolves parliament before a general election.
- When a bill is passed by parliament, the monarch formally agrees it – when it is given the royal assent. This changes a bill into an Act of Parliament, making it a law.
- Over hundreds of years the power of the monarchy has been transferred to the elected government.
- Some countries still have a system of government based upon the monarch having absolute power.

House of Commons
- Elected chamber of 650 members.
- The government is formed based on the elections held to this chamber.
- The prime minister and most government ministers are members of this House.
- Votes the policy of the government into legislation.
- The will of the House of Commons is always supreme.
- The Commons sees its role as holding the government to account for its actions, debating and amending bills and being a forum for national debate.

House of Lords
- Over 1,000 appointed life peers and some hereditary peers and bishops of the Church of England.
- Its role is to debate and revise legislation from the House of Commons.
- It can also propose legislation (normally about uncontroversial issues).
- It carries out scrutiny functions similar to the House of Commons.
- There are joint committees of both Houses.

Figure 7.1 The nature of bicameral Westminster parliament

Check your understanding and progress at **www.hoddereducation.co.uk/myrevisionnotes**

Tip

Remember, bicameral mean two parts. Draw a simple sketch of the Westminster Parliament, divided into two parts – the House of Lords and House of Commons. Write down the features of each in the correct place, such as elected, non-elected, MPs most powerful, lifetime appointments, the Speaker, etc.

The UK's major political parties

REVISED

A brief history of UK party politics

+ The party political system in the UK dates back to the mid-nineteenth century, when the political divide was between the Whigs and the Tories. In the late 1800s these two informal groups became established national political parties – the Liberals and the Conservatives.
+ From 1900, a third party emerged established by the trade union movement – the Labour Party.
+ After the First World War, the Liberals went into decline and a two-party system emerged made up of the Conservative and Labour parties.
+ From the mid-1970s onwards the make-up of parliament began to involve a wider range of parties, including the Scottish and Welsh Nationalists and a number of parties from Northern Ireland. The Liberal Party merged with the SDP and is now known as the Liberal Democrats.
+ More recently the Green Party has emerged as a national force.

Political ideology

+ Ideology refers to a system of ideas and ideals. The ideology of each political party determines the way it approaches political issues.
+ Political parties are referred to as being to the left, right or centre (see Figure 7.2).

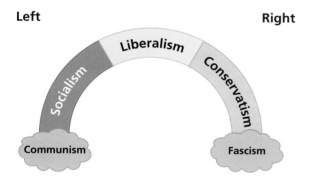

Left   **Right**

Liberalism
Socialism   Conservatism
Communism   Fascism

Figure 7.2 Parties are traditionally described as right, left or centre

The political ideologies associated with the main UK political parties are:
+ Socialism – associated with the Labour Party, based on common ownership, a belief in community and equality. It ranges from communism to social democracy.
+ Conservatism – associated with the Conservative Party, based upon tradition, duty and authority and property. It encompasses views from Tory paternalism to the New Right.
+ Liberalism – was associated with the Liberal Democrats, concerned with human rights and individual liberty, freedom and tolerance, and consent. Modern liberalism differs from classical liberalism due to a greater emphasis on social and welfare issues.

Table 7.4 illustrates the key policy pledges of political parties during the 2019 general election.

Table 7.4 Key policy pledges of political parties in 2019

Policy	Conservative Party pledge	Labour Party pledge	Liberal Democrat Party pledge
Brexit	Get Brexit done without any delay.	Renegotiate the terms of a deal with the EU.	Hold a new referendum to remain in the EU.
NHS	50,000 new nurses, 40 new hospitals.	Increase spending by 4.3% per year.	1p extra on income tax to go to the NHS.
Taxation	No increases in income tax, NI or VAT.	Raise tax for those on £80K or more.	Replace business rates, increase corporation tax to 20%.
Economy	Make free trade agreements with other countries. Retake World Trade Organization seat. Support start-up and small businesses.	Nationalise the Royal Mail, buses, water and energy. Set up a National Investment Bank.	Invest £130bn in transport, energy, schools and homes.

Activity

Make sure you keep up to date with the policies of different UK political parties by frequently visiting their websites:

Conservative Party: **www.conservatives.com/**

Labour Party: **https://labour.org.uk/**

Liberal Democrat Party: **www.libdems.org.uk/**

Green Party: **https://vote.greenparty.org.uk/**

How parliament works

REVISED

Parliament works by holding the government to account for its actions in several ways (see Figure 7.3).

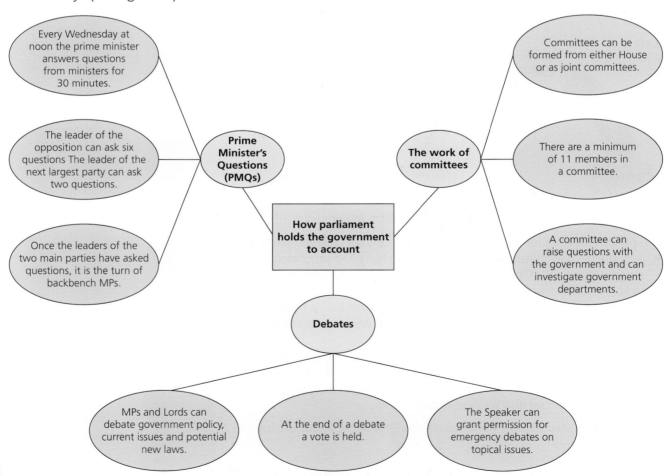

Figure 7.3 How parliament holds the government to account

Check your understanding and progress at **www.hoddereducation.co.uk/myrevisionnotes**

The role of Members of Parliament

REVISED ⬤

+ Members of Parliament (MPs) are elected to represent a constituency and all the people who live in the constituency.
+ MPs divide their time between working in parliament, in their constituency and working for their political party.
+ Some MPs hold ministerial posts or shadow ministerial posts with specific responsibilities, which take up a lot of their time.
+ Some MPs also have other jobs and paid and unpaid outside interests, such as writing, belonging to pressure or campaign groups, or advising outside bodies. All of these now have to be registered and the details are made public.

MPs' salaries

+ The annual salary of an MP (in 2022) was £84,114 and they are also allowed to claim living expenses and office costs.
+ The prime minister (in 2022) was paid £159,554 per year.
+ Government ministers also receive an additional salary on top of their MPs' salary.
+ The leader of the opposition and the opposition chief whip also receive an additional salary.

The work of MPs in parliament

+ When parliament is in session, MPs spend a lot of their time working in the House of Commons. This work includes:
  + dealing with constituency correspondence and issues
  + raising issues affecting their constituents
  + attending debates and voting on new laws
  + speaking in the House of Commons
  + attending functions both relating to their party politics and their political interests.
+ Most MPs are also members of select or standing committees, which look at issues of government policy or new laws.

Working in constituencies

+ Many MPs leave the House on Thursdays and return to their constituencies.
+ They hold 'surgeries' where they meet constituents and discuss their problems.
+ They also attend a number of functions, from school and local business events to party-political functions in their constituency.

Helping constituents

+ A local MP is there to assist all constituents with their problems.
+ Many problems that MPs deal with are confidential and are not made public.
+ An MP may write to the government department or meet a minister on a constituent's behalf to resolve an issue.

61

+ If it is an issue that can be made public, the MP can raise it in the House of Commons where it becomes a part of the official record and can come to the attention of the media.
+ A constituent may give their MP the authority to raise the issue outside parliament, to seek publicity for the issue. MPs can also raise issues by:
  + asking questions of ministers or the prime minister
  + adjournment debates – held for 30 minutes at the end of each day (members can raise any issue in this debate)
  + backbench debates – an MP can ask that the issue be raised in the time allocated for backbench debates (35 days a year are set aside for these debates)
  + a Private Members' Bill (PMB) – an MP can put their name forward for the PMB ballot that is held each year. If their name comes up near the top of the list and the issue they want to raise is uncontroversial, they stand a reasonable chance of introducing a bill that will become law.

Scrutiny role

MPs also have an important role to scrutinise proposed legislation, both on the floor of the House and in committee. This work is more fully outlined in the section about legislation (see page 63).

> **Activity**
>
> Contact your local MP and ask them: to visit your school, for information about an issue you are investigating, for their views on a topic. You can usually find out about the work they are undertaking on their website.

Key parliamentary roles

REVISED ⬤

There are a number of roles carried out that are necessary to the operation of our democratic process and the workings of parliament (see Table 7.5).

Table 7.5 Parliamentary roles

Parliamentary role	Commentary
The Speaker	The Speaker of the House of Commons is elected to the post by their fellow MPs.
	Chairs debates in the Commons Chamber.
	The chief officer and has the highest authority in the Commons.
	Interprets the rules of the House.
	Can bar members, decide who speaks and call ministers to the House to make statements.
	There are three Deputy Speakers who can also chair sittings of the House. They are also elected by their fellow MPs.
	Once elected, these MPs withdraw from any active political role.
Lord Speaker	Elected by members of the House of Lords.
	Politically impartial, they are responsible for chairing the debates in the Lords chamber and offering advice on procedure.
Whips	MPs or Members of the House of Lords appointed by each party in parliament to help organise parliamentary business and to ensure that their party's MPs turn out and vote according to the party's wishes.
	Every week, whips send out a notice to their MPs and the Lords giving instructions on how to vote.
Frontbench MPs	**Frontbenchers** are ministers who sit on the benches nearest to the Speaker in the House of Commons.
	On the government side these are ministers and on the opposition side these are shadow ministers representing the official opposition party sit.

Check your understanding and progress at **www.hoddereducation.co.uk/myrevisionnotes**

Table 7.5 *continued*

Parliamentary role	Commentary
Backbench MPs	A **backbencher** is an ordinary MP who holds no government or opposition post.
	Sit behind the front bench on the backbenches.
Black Rod	A senior officer in the House of Lords, responsible for its security and for the major ceremonial events at the Palace of Westminster.

The legislative process

REVISED

Types of legislation

Parliament deals with a range of different types of laws. Bills (draft legislation) can be introduced by:

+ the government
+ individual MPs or Lords
+ private individuals or organisations.

There are four different types of bill:

+ Public bills: change the law as it applies to the entire population and are the most common type of bill. They are proposed by government ministers.
+ Private bills: usually promoted by organisations like local authorities or private companies, to give them additional powers. They only change the law in regard to that one organisation or body.
+ Hybrid bills: a mix of the characteristics of public and private bills. The changes to the law proposed by a hybrid bill would affect the general public, but they would also have a significant impact on specific individuals or groups, for example, the construction of the HS2 rail line.
+ Private Members' Bills: a form of public bill as they affect the entire population, but they cannot involve raising taxation. They are introduced by MPs and Lords who are not government ministers. They often relate to social issues, for example, abortion, divorce or sexuality.

Making laws

In order to become a law, an idea must be set out in writing. It then goes through various parliamentary stages before it is signed into law by the monarch. These stages are shown in Figure 7.4.

The Green Paper
Often the Government will publish a 'Green Paper', which is a discussion document about a possible new law, and invite MPs and others to comment upon its suggestions. It is called Green because the cover is green.

The First Reading
The Government then publishes a 'White Paper', which is a proposal for a new law. This becomes a Bill (draft law) and is formally announced (First Reading) in the House of Commons. No debate takes place at this time.

The Second Reading
This stage involves a debate upon the principle of the proposed legislation and a vote takes place at the end of the debate.

The Committee Stage
This stage comes next, where a group of MPs from all parties discuss the Bill in detail, line by line, and vote on amendments.

The Report Stage
The work of the committee is discussed and voted upon in the House of Commons.

The Third Reading (or Final Stage)
The amended legislation is voted upon and the legislation is then sent to the House of Lords where all the same stages from First Reading to Third Reading are gone through. If the Lords make amendments, the Bill returns to the House of Commons where further votes take place until the Bill is accepted.

The Royal Assent
The legislation then receives Royal Assent – it is agreed and signed by the monarch – and then becomes Law.

Figure 7.4 How a bill becomes law

Government formation

REVISED

+ When a general election is called all MPs stand down and become, if they wish, candidates for election.
+ The prime minister and other ministers, while no longer MPs, remain in post so the work of government can continue.
+ After the results are known the existing prime minister goes to Buckingham Palace to inform the monarch:
  + that their party has won, and the monarch should ask them to form a new government
  + that their party has lost, and the monarch should ask the leader of the majority party to form a government
  + that no party has won a majority.

+ In theory the monarch can ask anyone to form a government, but over time the convention described above has evolved.

Government formation examples

+ Coalition: in the **2010** general election Prime Minister Gordon Brown did not win a majority of the seats and was unable to form a government. Conservative Party leader David Cameron therefore formed a coalition government with the Liberal Democrats, which gave the coalition a reasonable majority in the House of Commons.
+ Lost majority: in the **2017** general election the Conservatives lost their majority but were still the largest party. Theresa May remained as prime minister and made a parliamentary deal with the Democratic Unionist Party (DUP) to ensure a parliamentary majority.
+ Latest election: in **2019** Prime Minister Boris Johnson, with the support of other parties, called a December general election. He campaigned on the slogan 'Get Brexit done'. The Conservatives won an overall majority of 80 seats. Labour Party leader Jeremy Corbyn stood down after the election when his party came third in the vote, while Jo Swinson quit as leader of the Liberal Democrats when she lost her seat.

The prime minister and cabinet

 REVISED

The role of the prime minister

The prime minister:
+ is the leader of their political party and responsible for its operation
+ is head of government, responsible for appointing the cabinet and junior ministers
+ is increasingly seen as the spokesperson for the UK abroad and at international events and summits
+ is responsible and accountable to parliament for the actions of the government
+ is often the spokesperson for the nation during times of crisis
+ is still a constituency MP carrying out the normal duties of an MP
+ holds weekly meetings with the monarch
+ chairs cabinet meetings.

The prime minister's powers

The prime minister:
+ appoints the cabinet and numerous other governmental and non-governmental posts
+ decides the date of a general election
+ gives direction to government policy
+ sums up cabinet debate so therefore states what is happening within government
+ removes ministers and other government appointees and replaces them with new people.

Differing prime ministerial styles

+ 'First among equals' has been used to describe the role of the prime minister. This implies that the prime minister is one of a team – that is, the cabinet – and that the cabinet is of equal importance to the prime minister. The phrase 'cabinet government' is often used to describe how the British system of government operates.
+ Recently, many prime ministers have been described as 'presidential' in the way they work.
+ Tony Blair, prime minister from 1997 to 2008, operated a 'sofa-style government' during which decisions were made often by small groups without civil servants present.

Cabinet and ministers

+ The current cabinet consists of 21 members, usually senior ministers, and there are a further 97 junior ministers.
+ The size of the cabinet is not limited, but the number that can have a ministerial salary is.
+ The senior posts within the cabinet are traditionally:
  + chancellor of the exchequer
  + foreign secretary
  + home secretary
  + defence secretary.
+ Each government department includes a senior minister and a number of junior ministers who cover areas of the department's work, and members of the House of Lords who answer departmental questions in the Lords.
+ When members of the cabinet agree on important issues, they are then held to the concept of 'collective responsibility' to support the policy even if they personally do not agree with it.

Government departments, agencies and the civil service

REVISED ●

Government departments

+ Ministers attend cabinet meetings and also each run a government department supported by a number of junior ministers.
+ Government ministers who are accountable to parliament run the government.
+ There are also numerous agencies and other public bodies and high-profile groups, public corporations, and the three devolved administrations that also work with the UK government departments.
+ The structure can vary from government to government. Departments can be renamed, merged or disappear.

Agencies

+ Agencies are business units that take on specific services on behalf of their associated government department. For example, the Driver and Vehicle Licensing Agency (DVLA) is the agency of the transport department.
+ The term used to cover the range of differing agency arrangements is non-departmental public bodies (NDPBs).
+ They are also known by the term 'quango' (quasi autonomous non-governmental organisations).

The civil service

+ The civil service helps the government develop and implement its policies.
+ It also provides services directly to the public, including running prisons, employment services, and the benefits and pension system.
+ In recent years, government policy has been to reduce civil service numbers. According to the Institute for Government, between 2010 and 2016, the size of the civil service fell by 19 per cent, but numbers have risen since the EU referendum as policy specialists were recruited to deal with the heavy workload caused by Brexit and the Covid-19 pandemic.
+ Civil servants are politically neutral, impartial and remain in post when governments change.
+ They are also anonymous to the public, but increasingly those in NDPBs are becoming accountable and are often called before parliamentary committees.
+ Each government appoints a number of special advisers, political appointees who advise ministers on policy issues. While in post they are employed as temporary civil servants.

✚ The Senior Civil Service (SCS) is made up of the top 4,000 civil servants who devise policy and advise ministers. Civil servants in this group earn in the range of £150,000 to £288,000.

✚ In 2021 there were 484,880 full-time equivalent (FTE) civil service employees.

Tip

It is not necessary to remember the names of actual government ministers. Instead, focus on the range of posts within government, especially the three most senior cabinet posts.

Useful websites

BBC News: **www.bbc.co.uk/news/election/2019/results**

The British Monarchy: **www.royal.gov.uk**

Courts and Tribunals Judiciary: **www.judiciary.gov.uk**

Electoral Reform Society: **www.electoral-reform.org.uk**

Full list of cabinet members: **www.gov.uk/government/ministers**

Government structure: **www.gov.uk/government/organisations**

House of Lords: **www.parliament.uk/lords**

MPs' pay and expenses: **www.parliament.uk/about/mps-and-lords/members/pay-mps/**

Prime Minister's Office: **www.gov.uk/government/organisations/prime-ministers-office-10-downing-street**

Register of Members' Financial Interests: **www.publications.parliament.uk/pa/cm/cmregmem.htm**

Supreme Court: **www.supremecourt.uk**

UK government: **www.gov.uk**

UK Parliament: **www.parliament.uk**

Key points check

Can you answer the key points related to this chapter? If you are unclear about how to respond to any of these questions, revisit the relevant topics in the chapter.

✚ How do elections work in the UK?

✚ How do the different voting systems work?

✚ How does the UK's two-chamber parliament work?

✚ What political parties exist in the UK?

✚ How does the government work and pass laws?

Now test yourself (AO1)   TESTED

1 Name one type of peer who sits in the House of Lords.

2 Identify one of the most senior cabinet posts.

3 Name an electoral voting system used in the UK.

4 Define what is meant by the term 'coalition government'.

5 Explain the role of the Speaker in the House of Commons.

6 Identify a general election in which no party won an overall majority.

Exam practice

1 Using Table 7.1 on page 56, which shows the number of MPs elected in the 2019 general election and each party's national vote, describe the options for forming the new government if the election had been based upon a proportional voting system. [4] (AO2)

2 Analyse the main policy differences between the major parties at the 2019 general election. [8] (AO3)

3* If you were an active citizen wishing to bring about a change in government policy, examine whether you would be more likely to succeed were you a member of a pressure group or a backbench MP.

In your answer you should consider:
+ the ways in which pressure groups operate
+ the opportunities for backbench MPs to bring about change. [8] (AO3)

Remember, the * means this is a synoptic question, which draws upon your knowledge and understanding from more than one theme. You can find more information on page 10.

Elections to the European Parliament

+ In 2016 a referendum resulted in the UK voting to leave the European Union (EU).
+ From 1979 until 2019 voters in the UK took part in elections to the European Parliament.
+ Elections for the European Parliament are held every five years.
+ The next elections are due in 2024.
+ Member countries must use a proportional system of voting to elect members of the European Parliament. This system ensures that a range of views are represented in the parliament.
+ The type of proportional voting system varies between each member country.
+ Voters in European elections often vote on national issues and against their own government of the time, rather than on transnational European issues.
+ In the European Parliament, Members of the European Parliament (MEPs) sit in transnational groups each made up of at least 23 MEPs from a quarter of the member states.
+ The parliament sits in a horseshoe design by party group, like many continental parliaments.

> **Tip**
>
> Remember, the European Parliament is not as powerful as most national parliaments.

Figure 8.1 illustrates the size of political groups that sit in the European Parliament in 2019–24, while Figure 8.2 shows the proportion of members from each political group.

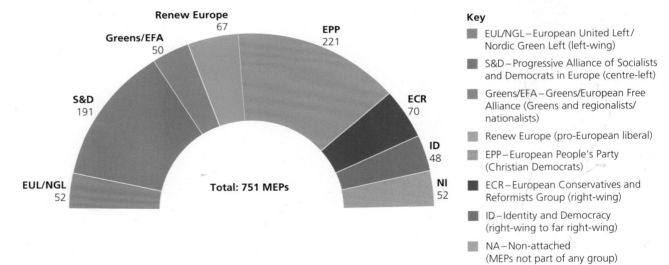

Key
- EUL/NGL – European United Left/Nordic Green Left (left-wing)
- S&D – Progressive Alliance of Socialists and Democrats in Europe (centre-left)
- Greens/EFA – Greens/European Free Alliance (Greens and regionalists/nationalists)
- Renew Europe (pro-European liberal)
- EPP – European People's Party (Christian Democrats)
- ECR – European Conservatives and Reformists Group (right-wing)
- ID – Identity and Democracy (right-wing to far right-wing)
- NA – Non-attached (MEPs not part of any group)

Figure 8.1 The size of political groups in the European Parliament, 2019–24

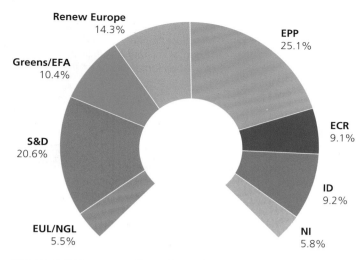

Figure 8.2 The proportion of members from each political group in the European Parliament, 2019–24

Political systems outside the UK

Many countries have 'democratic' in their name or describe themselves as democratic, but they do not meet the demands set out in earlier chapters and outlined in Figure 5.1 on page 34 of what truly makes a democratic society.

> **Tip**
>
> To assist your revision, copy the headings in Figure 8.3 and choose a country you think is **non-democratic**. Check it against the criteria identified in the figure and shown in Figure 5.1 on page 34 regarding what makes a democracy.

Absolute monarchy – a traditional form of government in which power is held by one family based upon a hereditary principle of power being transferred down a royal line. A small number of countries still have an absolute monarchy. Most monarchies now are called constitutional monarchies, where the monarch has passed all or most of their powers to an elected government and the monarch is a symbol of national unity. The UK is an example of a constitutional monarchy. Examples of absolute monarchies are Brunei, Oman, Qatar, Saudi Arabia, Eswatini (Swaziland).

Authoritarian rule – where power is in the hands of a leader or a small group that is not constitutionally accountable to the people. Authoritarian leaders rule outside the existing laws and legal framework. Citizens do not normally have a chance to free themselves of their rule by the electoral process. This form of rule is often seen when the military takes over a state. For example, the current government in Egypt was formed after a military takeover. Although after the takeover a President was elected, because he was the ex-military chief and because of the circumstances of the election and the situation in Egypt, there is a system of authoritarian rule in place.

Dictatorship – a system of government where there is rule by one person or group. In 2020, according to Freedom House there were 50 dictatorships in the world. There are 19 in Sub-Saharan Africa, 12 in the Middle East and North Africa, eight in Asia-Pacific, seven in Eurasia, three in the Americas and one in Europe. Examples include Belarus, Cuba and Laos. Many dictators also happen to be absolute monarchs or heads of single-party states.

Oligarchy – a system whereby the control of the state and economy is by a small group of well-placed, extremely wealthy insiders. These people could be formed from royalty or the wealthy, due to family ties, education or corporate power, or from the military. This system can sit alongside differing forms of democracy. It is often used to describe how the Russian system of government works alongside the elected government members.

Figure 8.3 Democracy checklist (*continues on next page*)

Technocracy – a government system based upon people who are not elected but are technical experts in their field. A recent example would be in Ukraine in 2019, where newly elected former comedian President Volodymyr Zelensky called on the other parliamentary parties to contribute names of candidates for building a technocratic government.

Military dictatorship – where the government is run by the military. The phrase 'military junta' is often used to describe the group of military officers running a country. Examples of military juntas are Myanmar and Sudan.

Aristocracy – government by the few, usually based upon inherited wealth and status in society. In the UK for many centuries this power of the nobility/aristocracy worked alongside the power of the monarch.

Theocracy – where the government of the state is held by religious figures whose beliefs dominate the governmental system. Examples are Iran and the Vatican.

One-party state – a system that allows only one political party to hold power. There may be elections, but the candidates will belong to the one party and there may be no choice of candidates on the ballot paper. Examples of one-party states are China, Cuba, Eritrea, Laos, Vietnam and Western Sahara.

Figure 8.3 Democracy checklist (*continued*)

Useful websites

Amnesty International: **www.amnesty.org/en/countries/**

European Parliament: **www.europarl.europa.eu/portal/en**

Freedom House: **www.freedomhouse.org**

Global Witness: **www.globalwitness.org/en**

Key points check

Can you answer the key points related to this chapter? If you are unclear about how to respond to any of these questions, revisit the relevant topics in the chapter.

✚ How does the European Parliament electoral system differ from the UK Parliament electoral system?
✚ What is the difference between a democratic and a non-democratic system?

Now test yourself (AO1)

TESTED

1 Identify one important characteristic of a democracy.
2 Define, using an example, what is meant by 'absolute monarchy'.
3 What type of voting system is used for elections to the European Parliament?
4 What is a 'theocracy'?
5 Explain the composition of a transnational political group in the European Parliament.
6 Name a country that can be described as having a military dictatorship.

Exam practice

1   Figures 8.1 and 8.2 on pages 68 and 69 show the composition of the
    European Parliament. Describe in what ways the layout and composition
    of the European Parliament differ from that of the current UK Parliament.
    Refer to the figures in your answer.   [4] (AO2)

2   Justify the claim that the UK is a fully functioning democracy.   [8] (AO3)

3* To what extent is it important that in a democracy the rights of the media
    and the press are safeguarded?

    In your answer you should consider:
    +   the role of the media in society
    +   the relationship between a political system and the media.   [8] (AO3)

Remember, the * means this is a synoptic question, which draws upon your
knowledge and understanding from more than one theme. You can find more
information on page 10.

My Revision Notes: AQA GCSE (9–1) Citizenship Studies

9 What are the principles and values that underpin British society? (3.2.1)

The key principles and values underpinning British society

REVISED

+ A society's values are based upon its culture, religion and history.
+ The Universal Declaration of Human Rights (UDHR) identifies values and principles that are now seen as universal – see page 123.

British values

+ British values came onto the political agenda in the early 2000s due to:
    + the increased terror threat to the UK
    + the debate around the increase in migration to the UK
    + the success of policies related to multiculturalism.
+ In 2014 the British government announced that schools were required to promote British values (see Figure 9.1).

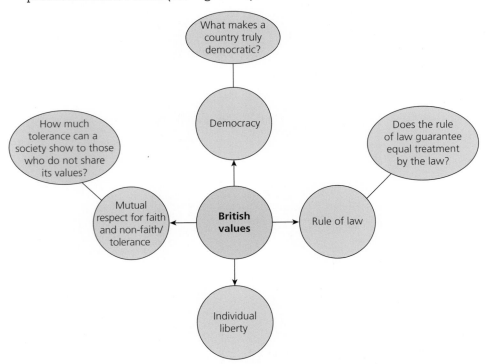

Figure 9.1 The fundamental British values according to the Department for Education (DfE)

The rights, duties and freedoms of citizens

REVISED

+ While we use the phrases rights, responsibilities, freedoms and the rule of law in everyday conversation in regard to citizenship, they have exact meanings.
+ There are often debates within society about the balance between rights and duties or responsibilities, for example, during times of war or a pandemic.

Check your understanding and progress at **www.hoddereducation.co.uk/myrevisionnotes**

+ What rights should citizens have and what duties or responsibilities can the state expect from its citizens? For example, in a time of war the state increases the duties it places upon its citizens, from calling up people to fight to rationing food and limiting citizens' rights, such as freedom of movement and speech.

Table 9.1 summarises the rights, duties and freedoms of citizens in the UK. Note, these elements cross-reference many other sections of the course and the outline indicated here is developed in other sections of the book.

Table 9.1 The rights, duties and freedoms of citizens

Term	Meaning
Rights	The legal binding, social and ethical entitlements that are considered the building blocks of a society.
	All citizens within our society enjoy them equally.
	The idea of freedom of speech is an essential part of our way of life, but society does limit that right where your individual rights conflict with other rights.
	Rights within a society structure the way government operates, the content of laws and the morality of society.
	Rights are often grouped together and debates take place about human rights or children's rights or prisoners' rights, for example.
Morals	The rules that govern which actions are believed to be right and which are wrong.
	They are often related to personal behaviour.
	A society can claim to live by certain moral values.
	Individuals can state that they live their life by certain moral values.
Duties and responsibilities	Duties and responsibilities are placed upon citizens by society. For example, you are expected to pay your taxes, obey the law and take part in the judicial system as a jury member if required.
	Duties are not optional and are often enshrined in law.
Freedoms	The power or right to speak and act as or think as one wants.
	We often explain freedom in relation to a context. Expressions like: freedom of choice, the freedom of the press and freedom of movement relate to some basic beliefs in our society.
Equality	Treating all individuals equally.
	Where inequality or discrimination occurs the state often attempts to remedy the situation through either policy or legislative action.

Duties and responsibilities

The terms 'duties' and 'responsibilities' are often interchangeable, but 'duty' often implies a legal or moral underpinning.

Tip

It is helpful to answer any questions about such terms by using an example to indicate your ability to both understand the question and apply your knowledge to a real-life situation.

Key equality and rights legislation

Rights of women

+ Representation of the People (Equal Franchises) Act 1928: granted equal voting rights to women and men. It gave the vote to all women over 21 years old, regardless of property ownership. Prior to this act only women over 30 who met minimum property qualifications could vote.
+ Equal Pay Act 1970: made it unlawful to pay women less than men for doing the same work.
+ Equality Act 2010: brought together a number of existing laws. The law protects against discrimination on the grounds of the 'protected characteristics' of age, disability, gender reassignment, marriage and civil partnership, pregnancy and maternity, race, religion or belief, sex and sexual orientation.
+ Sex Discrimination Act 1975: made it unlawful to discriminate in the workplace because of one's gender or marital status.

73

Racial equality

+ Race Relations Acts 1965, 1968, 1976 and 2000.
+ The 1965 Act banned racial discrimination in public places and made the promotion of hatred on the grounds of 'colour, race, or ethnic or national origins' an offence.

Rights of the child

+ The United Nations Convention on the Rights of the Child (UNCRC) came into force in 1992. Every child in the UK is entitled to over 40 specific rights.

Sexual rights

+ Sexual Offences Act 1967: decriminalised homosexual behaviour between adults.
+ Civil Partnership Act 2005: allowed same sex couples to register their civil partnership.
+ Sexual Offences Act 2003: partly replaced the earlier 1956 Act and created several new sexual offences.
+ Gender Recognition Act 2004: made provision for individuals with gender dysphoria to change their legal gender.
+ Marriage (Same Sex Couples) Act 2013: introduced same sex marriage in England and Wales.

Race audit

In 2017 the government published consolidated data for the first time that indicated the experience of public services by different racial groups in the UK. The government stated that the information contained in the data may lead to changes in legislation to attempt to overcome some of the issues raised.

To find out more about what these data tell us about the UK today use the following website: **www.ethnicity-facts-figures.service.gov.uk**.

Key factors that create individual, group, national and global identities

REVISED ●

The factors that form identity are multidimensional and they influence different individuals in different ways (see Table 9.2).

Table 9.2 Some of the factors that affect individual, group, national and global identities

Identity	Factors	Comments
Individual	Gender	The extent of the effect of these factors varies depending on the individual.
	Race	
	Family	
	Ethnic group	
	Social class	
	Religion	
	Education	
	Employment	
	Peer group	
	Location	
	Culture	
	Media	

Check your understanding and progress at **www.hoddereducation.co.uk/myrevisionnotes**

Table 9.2 *continued*

Identity	Factors	Comments
Group	Employment Peer group Social interests Political views	Within a group context individuals can be influenced by the identity of the group.
National	Shared values	**National identity** and its association with national values should not be confused with national characteristics and stereotyping. Factors influencing national identity could be, for example, the sense of patriotism and continuity created by a country's monarchy.
Global	Political, social and environmental awareness	Increasingly in this interconnected world of 24-hour news, individuals can readily identify with global issues and concerns.

Useful websites

Government ethnicity facts and figures: **www.ethnicity-facts-figures.service.gov.uk**

Office for National Statistics (ONS): www.ons.gov.uk

Process of applying to become a UK citizen: **www.gov.uk/becoming-a-british-citizen/check-if-you-can-apply**

Young Citizens – British values: **www.youngcitizens.org/resources/citizenship/british-values/**

Key points check

Can you answer the key points related to this chapter? If you are unclear about how to respond to any of these questions, revisit the relevant topics in the chapter.
+ What are the key values and principles that underpin British society?
+ What are the main factors that help determine a person's identity?

Now test yourself (AO1)

TESTED

1. Name one factor that influences an individual's identity.
2. Identify one type of group identity.
3. Define what is meant by the term 'equality'.
4. Explain, using an example, how the government has tried to overcome inequality in society.
5. Identify one key British value.
6. Define what is meant by a citizen's duties.

Source A: division of wealth in the UK

Wealth differences in the UK

- Latest government data show that the top 10% of wealthy people in the UK own 43% of the country's wealth.
- The bottom 50% of the population own 9% of the country's wealth.
- The richest 1% of the population each have personal wealth of at least £3.6m.
- The 10% least wealthiest in the UK each have personal wealth of no more than £15,500.
- Consider the factors that might impact on a person's identity if they are from the top 10% and the lowest 10% of wealthiest groups in the UK.

Figure 1

Source: adapted from www.hmrc.gov.uk/stats/personal_wealth/13-5-table-2005.pdf

1　How do you consider belonging to each of the four groups indicated in Figure 1 in Source A would impact upon a person's identity? 　[4] (AO2)

2　Make a case to justify the selection of the four fundamental British values identified by the UK government. 　[8] (AO3)

3*　Evaluate the case that states that the media are an important factor in influencing individual identity.

In your answer you should consider:
+ the range of factors than can influence individual identity
+ differing formats of the media and their influence. 　[8] (AO3)

Remember, the * means this is a synoptic question, which draws upon your knowledge and understanding from more than one theme. You can find more information on page 10.

10 What do we mean by identity? (3.2.2)

There are many ways we can study aspects of identity, from individual and group to societal. All three aspects are covered in this chapter.

The make-up of the UK and its impact on identity

It is important to understand the populations within each of the nations of the United Kingdom – England, Wales, Scotland and Northern Ireland (see Figure 10.1).

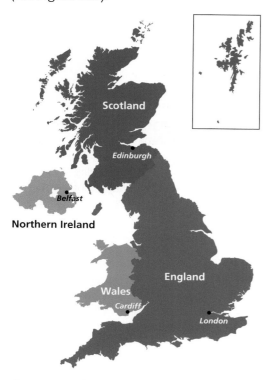

Figure 10.1 The nations of the UK

Table 10.1 shows that England is the dominant population of the UK, accounting for over 80 per cent of the population.

Table 10.1 Estimated and projected population of the UK and constituent countries, mid-2019 to mid-2043 (in millions)

	2019 (%)	2023*	2028*	2033*	2038*	2043*
United Kingdom	66.9 (100)	68.1	69.4	70.5	71.4	72.4
England	56.3 (84.3)	57.6	58.8	59.8	60.8	61.7
Scotland	5.5 (8.2)	5.5	5.5	5.6	5.6	5.6
Wales	3.2 (4.7)	3.2	3.2	3.2	3.2	3.3
Northern Ireland	1.9 (2.8)	1.9	2.0	2.0	2.0	2.0

* Projected

When considering population it is also important to understand the age structure of the population, both now and in future trends (see Table 10.2).

A nation with an ageing population faces different issues than one with a rising percentage of young people.

Table 10.2 Age distribution of the UK population, 1974 to 2039 (projected)

	% population aged 0 to 15	% population aged 16 to 64	% population aged 65 and over
1974	25.2	61.0	13.8
1984	21.0	64.1	14.9
1994	20.7	63.4	15.8
2004	19.5	64.5	15.9
2014	18.8	63.5	17.7
2024*	19.0	61.1	19.9
2034*	18.1	58.5	23.3
2039*	17.8	57.9	24.3

* Projected

+ Table 10.2 clearly shows that the percentage of young people in the UK is declining and is projected to decline in the future.
+ The percentage of people of working age is also declining.
+ The percentage of people aged over 60 is steadily increasing.

Each of these factors are influencing, and will continue to influence, decision-makers, politicians and voters for years to come.

How this affects identity debates

+ Identity within the nations and regions of the UK has historically been distinct, for example, Scotland has had its own education and legal systems.
+ National identity is shown in each nation's cultural identity and is based on literature, customs, music, language and sport. This varies between each nation.
+ Even within nations there are regional differences:
  + Northern Ireland has a divided cultural identity between those who are nationalist and support a united Ireland, and those who are unionist and support Northern Ireland and its union with the UK.
  + Within England, regions and counties have developed their own identities, such as Yorkshire, Lancashire and Cornwall.

The devolution of power

+ Until very recently the UK operated a very centralised state with all political power centred on London and the Westminster Parliament.
+ In recent years, debates around national identity have led to the growth of devolution of power to the nations and regions of the UK.
+ Scotland and Wales have their own parliaments and Northern Ireland has an assembly.
+ Devolved power means more decisions that impact upon the lives of people in the regions are decided by their own politicians in their own capital cities.

What questions does this raise about the UK?

+ Is there a clear perception of what it means to be British?
+ Do the British have a clear identity or does it come second to being Scottish, Welsh, Irish or English?
+ Will the recognition of separate national identities lead to the break-up of the UK?
+ Will Scotland vote to leave the union in a second referendum on independence?

Tip

While this topic involves an understanding of figures, what is important is not remembering statistics but being able to write about trends, and being able to draw together various figures to outline a case or make an argument. So don't get lost in numbers – just remember what picture the numbers paint.

Check your understanding and progress at **www.hoddereducation.co.uk/myrevisionnotes**

Changes and movement of the UK population over time

As well as noting at the differences between the populations of the four nations in the UK, we can also look at population changes in the UK over time, in terms of industrialisation and immigration.

The impact of the Industrial Revolution

+ In the nineteenth century the Industrial Revolution led to a large-scale movement of the UK population from the countryside to the towns. Many towns then grew into the large cities we have today.
+ Between 1771 and 1831 Manchester saw its population grow by 600 per cent.
+ Bradford's population grew by 50 per cent every ten years between 1811 and 1851.
+ More recently, many 'new towns' have been built to house the increasing population.
+ The fastest-growing cities between 2010 and 2020 were:
    + Coventry – 21.7 per cent
    + Exeter – 15.2 per cent
    + Edinburgh – 12.3 per cent
    + Peterborough – 11.4 per cent
    + London – 11.1 per cent

> **Activity**
>
> Using the internet, search for population data for your local community today and several hundred years ago. You can find the data via the Office for National Statistics (ONS) website and your local council.

The impact of immigration to the UK

The UK has been invaded and conquered, has conquered other countries and has accepted people from across the world to settle and live permanently in its individual nations.

Figure 10.2 shows some of the many groups of people who have settled in the UK over the centuries.

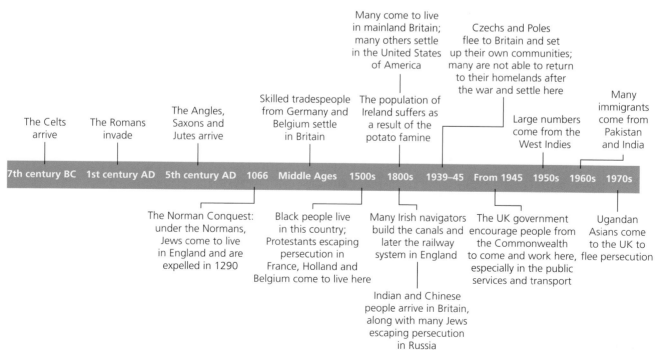

Figure 10.2 Changes to the population of the UK over time

- In the year ending June 2021:
  - 573,000 people migrated to (entered) the UK.
  - 334,000 people emigrated from (left) the UK.
  - This means that the net migration figure is 239,000 (the migration figure minus the emigration figure).
- In June 2021:
  - 6 million people living in the UK were foreign nationals – 9 per cent of the total population.
  - 3.4 million EU nationals were living in the UK.
  - As of 2019, 994,000 UK nationals were living in other EU countries (excluding Ireland).

Source: **https://commonslibrary.parliament.uk/research-briefings/sn06077/**

Figure 10.3 illustrates the total net migration in the UK between 2011 and 2020.

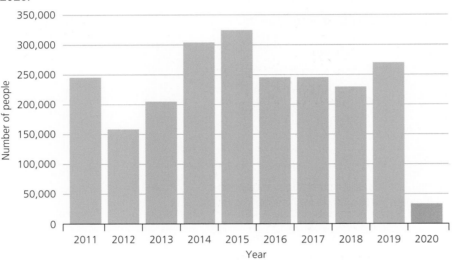

Figure 10.3 Total net migration, 2011 to 2020 (Net migration fell in 2020 due to the Covid-19 pandemic.)

Source: adapted from Office for National Statistics

Why people migrate to the UK

In 2020 the most common reasons for migration to the UK were:
- formal study – the most common main reason (36 per cent)
- work – the second most common reason (32 per cent).
- Other reasons given were to seek work and to join a family member.

Figure 10.4 illustrates the main reasons why people migrate to the UK.

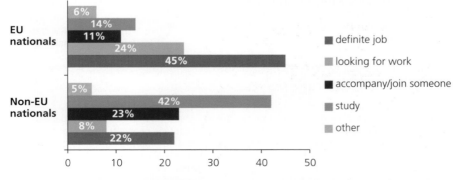

Figure 10.4 Reasons why people migrate to the UK

Arguments for and against immigration

Immigration to the UK continues to be a controversial issue. Table 10.3 outlines some of the arguments for and against immigration.

Check your understanding and progress at **www.hoddereducation.co.uk/myrevisionnotes**

Table 10.3 Arguments for and against immigration

Arguments in favour of immigration	Arguments against immigration
Cheap labour	Language problems
Helps overcome labour shortages	Can create ethnic and racial tensions
Immigrants are often prepared to do unskilled jobs	Jobs are lost to incoming workers
Some immigrants are highly skilled	By employing high-skilled migrant labour the government avoids the costs involved in developing the UK skills base
Cultural diversity	Pressure on housing and local services, especially where large numbers of migrants settle to work
Needed to fill places in the workforce	Immigrants may have limited skills and education

Mutual respect and understanding, and values, in a democratic and diverse society

REVISED

+ For many years, the agreement across UK political parties was that the UK aimed to be a multicultural society. This was understood as people from different places coming together to live in harmony and maintaining respect for their cultural and religious differences.
+ In 2011, Prime Minister David Cameron made a speech claiming that multiculturalism had failed because different groups were living separate lives within the UK.
+ Cameron believed the UK needed the following set of values to create a national identity:
  + freedom of speech
  + freedom of worship
  + democracy
  + the rule of law
  + equal rights regardless of race, sex or sexuality.
+ These are shared values associated with all Western liberal democracies and are included in human rights agreements.
+ To achieve this shared identity, Cameron believed the following practical things needed to be done:
  + immigrants should speak English
  + Britishness classes and British history should be taught in schools
  + a National Citizenship Service should be introduced for 16-year-olds
  + a 'Big Society' should be created which encouraged citizens to carry out voluntary work.

Limits to freedoms and values

It is important to remember that all of these freedoms and values have limits:

+ Freedom of speech: can you have complete freedom of speech? Can you say anything about anybody or anything? NO – there are legal limits.
+ Freedom of worship: there is freedom to worship and freedom not to worship. Society does not impose a set of religious beliefs on its citizens. The state does not allow the views of any religious group to be imposed upon society. This has caused protests recently in regard to cultural and educational issues.
+ Democracy: the choice of electoral system and voter or candidate qualifications can mean that many people feel unrepresented or that their vote doesn't count.
+ Rule of law: a citizen's ability to access legal processes is often limited by their lack of funds. The government limits the supports it gives to its citizens to bring legal cases.
+ Equal rights: groups and individuals often have to fight lengthy campaigns to overcome discrimination.

The future of multiculturalism

There are three possible paths suggested for the future of multiculturalism:

✤ Minority ethnic groups integrate into wider society. They begin to influence the dominant culture of the country, the culture evolves over time and cultural integration occurs.

✤ Minority ethnic groups integrate into society, adopting some aspects of the dominant culture while retaining their own culture. They live alongside the indigenous population.

✤ Minority ethnic groups do not integrate into wider society. They retain their own culture and reject the dominant culture.

Identity and multiple identities and the diverse nature of the UK population

REVISED ⬤

✤ A person's identity is made from various influences.

✤ There is a scientific discussion called the nature v. nurture debate which asks whether a person's development and identity depend more on their genetic inheritance or on their environment.

As Figure 10.5 shows, a range of factors impact upon individual identity.

✤ Group identity: the groups that a person is associated with. This could be a peer group – people your own age that you associate with; formal or informal groups; supporting a sports team; belonging to a voluntary group.

✤ Multiple identities: at different times in different situations, a person may adopt an identity based on a range of different aspects. For example, the Manchester City supporter who is second generation Pakistani, and supports Pakistan against England in a test cricket match.

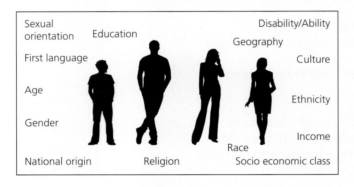

Figure 10.5 Are you able to construct a statement about your personal identity?

The diverse nature of the UK population

Table 10.4 indicates the distribution of the UK population by region and by country of birth.

Table 10.4 Estimated resident population of the UK by country of birth 2021 (%)

Region	UK	EU	Non-EU
England	**84**	**6**	**10**
North East	94	2	4
North West	90	4	6
Yorkshire and Humberside	90	4	6
East Midlands	87	5	7

→

Check your understanding and progress at **www.hoddereducation.co.uk/myrevisionnotes**

Table 10.4 *continued*

Region	UK	EU	Non-EU
West Midlands	86	5	10
East	87	6	7
London	63	11	26
South East	86	5	9
South West	91	4	5
Wales	**94**	**3**	**3**
Scotland	**90**	**5**	**5**
Northern Ireland	**92**	**5**	**3**
UK	**85**	**5**	**9**

Source: Sturge, G. (2022), 'Migration Statistics', House of Commons Library: **https:// researchbriefings.files.parliament.uk/documents/SN06077/SN06077.pdf**, page 25.

British identity

A survey found that the characteristics outlined in Figure 10.6 were considered important to possess in order to be described as British.

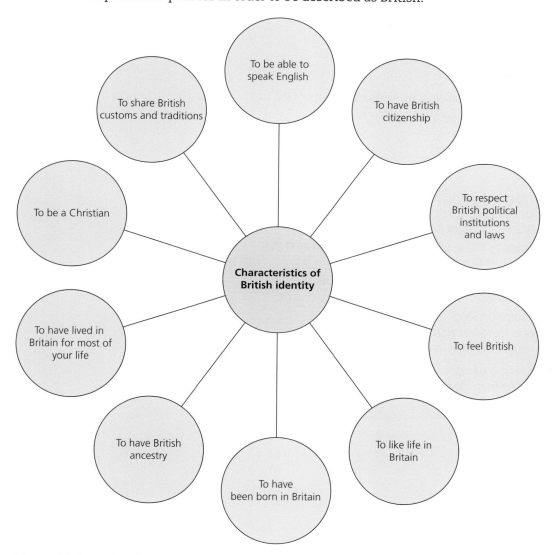

Figure 10.6 Results of a survey asking people what it means to be British

My Revision Notes: AQA GCSE (9–1) Citizenship Studies

Useful websites

British Social Attitudes Survey: **www.bsa.natcen.ac.uk/**

Migration Watch: **www.migrationwatchuk.org/statistics-net-migration-statistics**

Office for National Statistics – Population and Migration: **www.ons.gov.uk/peoplepopulationandcommunity/populationandmigration**

UK Parliament – Migration statistics (May 2022): **https://researchbriefings.files.parliament.uk/documents/SN06077/SN06077.pdf**

Key points check

Can you answer the key points related to this chapter? If you are unclear about how to respond to any of these questions, revisit the relevant topics in the chapter.
+ What factors and elements make up one's identity?
+ What is the make-up of modern UK society?
+ What freedoms and values do we associate with living in a democratic society?
+ What are the differing elements that can contribute to a person's identity?

Now test yourself (AO1)

TESTED

1 Identify two factors that can influence a person's identity.
2 Define what is meant by the term 'multiple identity'.
3 Identify one of the nations of the UK.
4 How does London differ in its population make-up to other parts of the UK?
5 Explain what is meant by the term 'net migration'.

Exam practice

1 Refer to Table 10.4 on pages 82–83, which shows the estimated resident population of the UK by country of birth. Discuss how issues relating to multiculturalism can differ in different parts of the UK. [4] (AO2)

2 Justify the argument made by Prime Minister David Cameron in 2011 that multiculturalism in the UK had failed. [8] (AO3)

3* Analyse the evidence that the growth of separate national identities in the UK will lead to the break-up of the UK as a state.

In your answer you should consider:
+ the nature of national identities within the UK
+ political developments that might lead to the break-up of the UK. [8] (AO3)

Remember, the * means this is a synoptic question, which draws upon your knowledge and understanding from more than one theme. You can find more information on page 10.

11 What is the role of the media and the free press? (3.2.3)

The role, rights and responsibilities of the media

REVISED

> **Tip**
>
> Do not confuse a 'free press' with free newspapers. Free newspapers are newspapers that are given away free of charge.

What do we mean by the media?

+ The term 'mass media' covers both traditional media in the form of newspapers and television, as well as new media in all their formats, such as social media.
+ The term 'citizen journalist' is used to describe the trend of individuals reporting on news events themselves, using their mobile phones and posting to social media platforms.

What are the rights of the media and free press?

+ In a democratic society the press has a right to be free from political and judicial interference and restrictions on the press should be as limited as possible.
+ While there is legislation ensuring television channels remain impartial, newspapers are able to support different political positions. During election campaigns, political parties look to newspapers to support their positions.

What is the role of the media in a modern society?

The media:
+ inform the public on what is going on (current affairs) and provide information on complex issues in an accessible way
+ encourage public debates on major issues of public concern
+ uncover abuses of power, challenge decision-makers and press for change
+ campaign and create and support public opinion in regard to issues and injustices
+ speak to those who hold positions of power (political, economic, social) so that they are both held to account and made aware of public opinion
+ ensure that a range of political views and opinions are made available to the public.

What are the responsibilities of the media towards society?

The media:
+ ensure that there is a balance between fact, analysis and opinion when reporting news
+ work in a professional manner, ensuring reporting is as accurate as possible

85

+ react to or set the political agenda and explain issues to enable the public to understand and participate in the debate
+ publish corrections and are held accountable for what is published
+ ensure that the public interest is a priority in both what is and what is not published, for example, they should not print information that could be harmful to national security or endanger individuals.

Case study

WikiLeaks

On 17 June 2022, Julian Assange – the founder of WikiLeaks, a website that publishes news leaks and classified media from anonymous sources – had his extradition to the US approved by the UK government. The US authorities want to place on him trial over the publication of leaked documents in 2010 and 2011 relating to the Iraq and Afghanistan wars, which the US claims broke the law and endangered lives.

Assange has fought against this extradition request for years, claiming it would be 'incompatible with his human rights' and that he would not be 'treated appropriately'.

This case brings into question the right of news outlets to publish leaked government documents they claim are in the public interest, while the government claims they are a threat to national security.

What must society do to ensure that there is freedom of the press?

Society must:
+ establish a legal and taxation framework that allows the media to thrive and survive
+ ensure that there is a legal and regulatory framework that encourages a range of views (plurality) and addresses issues such as the concentration of media ownership and ownership by non-UK individuals or companies, for example:
    + make available the necessary airwaves and infrastructure to allow for a range of media outlets
    + encourage both the private and public media sectors
    + ensure that all political parties have access to the media, especially during election campaigns
    + establish a legal framework that encompasses freedom of information laws but also legislates for privacy to provide a limit to media intrusion
    + create a regulatory framework that enables citizens, groups and organisations to hold the media accountable for their actions.

Media impact

It is important to consider the impact of the various media formats.
+ Social media and news on the internet can, by their nature, be seen, read and shared by millions of people within minutes.
+ Table 11.1 indicates the declining circulations of national newspapers in the UK. Most newspapers now have paid or open online platforms to ensure they operate a 24/7 news service as well as continuing to attract advertisers so that their businesses remain profitable.
+ Increasingly, young people use social media to obtain their news, often via influencers. In an age of increasing disinformation and news manipulation by governments, should the government take more action to regulate how people obtain their news?

Newspapers

The figures in Table 11.1 underestimate newspaper 'readership', as many people today consume their news through these newspapers' online outlets.

Check your understanding and progress at **www.hoddereducation.co.uk/myrevisionnotes**

Table 11.1 Chart indicating the declining circulation of national newspapers in the UK (in millions/m)

Newspaper	Party political leanings since 1980	July 1980	July 2011	January 2017	April 2022
The *Sun*	Has been both Labour and Conservative	3.7m	2.8m	1.7m	1.2m
Daily Mirror	Labour	3.6m	1.2m	0.7m	0.3m
Daily Mail	Conservative	1.9m	2.0m	1.5m	0.8m
Daily Telegraph	Conservative	1.4m	0.6m	0.5m	0.3m
The Times	Has been both Labour and Conservative	0.3m	0.4m	0.5m	0.3m
The *Guardian*	Labour/Liberal Democrat	0.4m	0.25m	0.15m	0.1m

Television

+ Table 11.2 indicates the number of viewers of television programmes in May 2022. Note that a news programme was at number 19 in this list.
+ These viewing figures are well down on numbers for past years. This is due to a greater choice of TV channels, the use of social media to gather news and the ability to watch programmes through on-demand streaming.

Table 11.2 Viewing figures for the top ten television programmes, May 2022

Programme	Channel	Number of viewers
Eurovision Song Contest	BBC 1	9,301,000
Britain's Got Talent	ITV	6,551,000
Queen's Platinum Jubilee Celebration	ITV	5,516,000
Coronation Street	ITV	5,334,000
FA Cup Final	BBC 1	5,230,000
Coronation Street	ITV	4,920,000

Source: **www.barb.co.uk/viewing-data/most-viewed-programmes/**

Social media

+ Out of the total estimated UK population of 67.9 million in 2020, approximately 44.84 million people are active Facebook users, or approximately 66 per cent of the population.
+ According to https://thesocialshepherd.com/blog/facebook-statistics, on average 1.62 billion users visit Facebook every day. That means that just under a quarter of the entire world population are daily active users!

Table 11.3 details the top ten Twitter accounts worldwide.

Table 11.3 The ten most followed Twitter accounts worldwide, August 2022

Name	Twitter handle	Number of followers
Barack Obama	@BarackObama	132,400,000
Justin Bieber	@justinbieber	114,100,000
Katy Perry	@katyperry	108,900,000
Rihanna	@rihanna	106,900,000
Elon Musk	@elonmusk	102,700,000
Cristiano Ronaldo	@Cristiano	102,600,000
Taylor Swift	@taylorswift13	90,800,000
Ariana Grande (before she deleted her account)	@ArianaGrande	85,300,000
Lady Gaga	@ladygaga	84,800,000
Narendra Modi	@narendramodi	81,300,000

Source: **www.tweetbinder.com/blog/top-twitter-accounts/**

Holding those in power to account

+ The media are one of the main ways in which those in power, be they politicians or those in business, are held to account.
+ Newspapers, television and the radio all carry out investigative journalism, through which they can hold those in power to account.
+ A recent example is the 2022 'Partygate' scandal, when parties were held in Downing Street during the Covid-19 restrictions. The media pursued the issue and it eventually led to a police investigation and a published Inquiry, which undermined the prime minister, Boris Johnson, and the government. This led to Johnson's resignation in July 2022.

> **Tip**
>
> Exam questions may relate to a specific media format, the role of the internet or the differences between television and newspaper news coverage, so make sure you focus on the media the question is asking you about rather than writing about the media in general. You can use the data in Tables 11.1 to 11.3 to show how the impact of various media formats has changed and is changing.

The right of the media to investigate and report on issues of public interest

REVISED

+ The UK media have the right to investigate and publish news stories they believe to be in the public interest.
+ The media have to balance freedom with their responsibility to ensure stories are accurate and protect individual privacy wherever possible.
+ There is a regulation structure for the media in order to maintain this balance.
+ If people believe they are inaccurately represented in the media they can use civil law to seek damages.
+ The Freedom of Information Act 2000 has given the media, and members of the public, the ability to gather information about public bodies. Case studies of how the media have prompted action by their investigative stories include the following:
  + In 2009, the *Guardian* led investigative reports into the now-defunct *News of the World* and other British newspapers owned by media mogul Rupert Murdoch, who it alleged had engaged in phone hacking of celebrities, members of the royal family and victims of crime as a means to gain private information. The resulting public outcry led to several convictions and a public inquiry into the scandal in 2011.
  + In 2000, after the murder of eight-year-old Sarah Payne, Sarah's parents launched a campaign calling for the government to make information about known local sex offenders available to the public. The campaign was backed by the *News of the World* and, in 2010, led parliament to roll out the scheme known as 'Sarah's Law' across England and Wales.

The operation of press regulation and examples of where censorship is used

REVISED

+ Press regulation in the UK is currently in a fluid situation. Following the phone hacking scandal in 2011 the government set up a Royal Commission. In 2012 the Commission published the Leveson Report, which recommended that a new body be established, backed up by legislation, to hold the industry to a new code of conduct.
+ Many newspaper owners and editors did not agree with recommendations of the Leveson Report.

- In response, in 2014 some newspapers set up the Independent Press Standards Organisation (IPSO), which handles complaints and investigates standards and compliance. It acts as a form of self-censorship.
- Over 1400 print titles have signed up to IPSO. The *Guardian*, the *Independent* and the *Financial Times* have not joined IPSO.
- It has already adjudicated in over 1000 complaints.

The government has now approved IMPRESS as the official press regulator but very few newspapers have signed up to be a part of its regulatory structure.

- IMPRESS maintains a Standards Code and assesses any breaches of this code by its members.
- It also provides an arbitration scheme that is free to the public and protects publishers against the risk of court costs and exemplary damages.

Censorship

- Censorship is the ability to suppress or prevent the publication of information.
- As well as censorship by outside bodies, the press themselves at times exercise self-censorship where they refuse to use materials they are offered either individually or collectively as an industry.

Censorship also exists in relation to other media formats:

- Films are classified as to their suitability for certain age groups by the British Board of Film Classification (BBFC). If they are not approved, they cannot be shown in British cinemas.
- The Broadcast Advertising Clearance Centre (BACC) approves all television advertising before it is shown.
- The Advertising Standards Authority (ASA) governs other advertising formats.
- Ofcom, a government body, has regulatory powers in regard to the media.
- The internet is currently not subject to formal legal regulation, although governments across the world are trying to introduce laws and regulations.
- Some countries ban access to some content and close down the internet completely for periods of time.

Examples of censorship issues
- The Terrorism Act 2006 made it an offence to 'glorify terrorism'. Some see this as a limit upon free speech.
- In 2013, the offices of the *Guardian* newspaper were raided by the police following the publication of stories about surveillance. The stories were based upon leaked material provided by Edward Snowden, a former National Security Agency (NSA) employee in the USA.
- In 2004, the *Observer* kept secret a memo it had allegedly showing that the UK had conducted a potentially illegal spying operation at the UN prior to the Iraq War.

Useful websites

Broadcasters' Audience Research Board (BARB): **www.barb.co.uk**

The *Guardian* – a news story about media ownership in the UK: **www.theguardian.com/media/2015/oct/21/uk-media-plurality-threatened-by-dominant-group-of-large-firms-report**

IMPRESS: **http://impress.press**

IPSO: **www.ipso.co.uk**

Newswhip – an account of the social media campaign in the 2017 general election: **www.newswhip.com/2017/06/labour-won-uks-social-media-election/**

Ofcom: **www.ofcom.org.uk**

Open Rights – a group that campaigns against potential internet censorship: **www.openrightsgroup.org/campaigns/**

Key points check

Can you answer the key points related to this chapter? If you are unclear about how to respond to any of these questions, revisit the relevant topics in the chapter.

+ What do we mean by the phrase 'the media'?
+ Why is it important to have a 'free press'?
+ What controls should operate with regard to the media?

Now test yourself (AO1)

TESTED

1 Define what is meant by the term 'censorship'.
2 Explain what is meant by the phrase 'in the public interest' regarding newspaper stories.
3 Identify one way in which the Freedom of Information Act 2000 aids journalists.
4 Name the regulatory body set up by most newspaper owners in 2014.
5 Why might a newspaper belong to IMPRESS rather than IPSO?

Exam practice

Source A: Chinese media control

The Chinese government has long kept a tight control on both traditional and new media to avoid potential challenge to its power and authority. Its tactics often mean strict media controls using monitoring systems and firewalls, shutting down publications or websites, and jailing dissident journalists, bloggers and activists. At the same time, the country's growing economy relies on the web for growth, and experts say the growing need for internet freedom is testing the regime's control.

1 Describe how the situation in the UK differs from that in China as described in Source A. [4] (AO2)

2 Examine why some people believe that the power of newspapers to influence public opinion is declining. [8] (AO3)

3* Justify the argument that politicians should pass laws to control and regulate the different forms of media that exist in the UK.

In your answer you should consider:
+ the different forms of the media that currently exist
+ the role of government in protecting its citizens. [8] (AO3)

Remember, the * means this is a synoptic question, which draws upon your knowledge and understanding from more than one theme. You can find more information on page 10.

Check your understanding and progress at **www.hoddereducation.co.uk/myrevisionnotes**

The role of the UK within international organisations

The key organisations identified within the specification are the:

✦ United Nations (UN)
✦ North Atlantic Treaty Organization (NATO)
✦ Council of Europe
✦ Commonwealth
✦ World Trade Organization (WTO)

The specification also identifies the European Union, although the UK is no longer a member.

The UN

✦ The UN was set up in 1945 following the end of the Second World War. Representatives of 51 countries met to draw up the United Nations Charter.
✦ The UN headquarters are in New York City.
✦ All members belong to the General Assembly, which debates and passes resolutions.
✦ The Security Council is made up of 15 members, five of which are permanent and have the ability to veto any proposals.
✦ The UN Charter sets out four purposes:
   1 To maintain international peace and security
   2 To develop friendly relations among nations
   3 To cooperate in solving international problems and in promoting respect for human rights
   4 To be a centre for harmonising the actions of nations.
✦ The Universal Declaration of Human Rights was adopted in 1948 (see page 123).
✦ Today, the UN is one of the most important international bodies in the world, with 193 members.

The UK's role in the UN

✦ The UK was a founder member of the UN.
✦ The UK is one of five permanent members of the Security Council – along with the USA, Russia, China and France. These countries can veto any decision.
✦ The UK's influence within the UN exceeds its economic or military influence. This is a good example of the UK's soft power.

UN agencies

The UN also operates a number of agencies to carry out its work, such as the:

✦ World Health Organization (WHO)
✦ International Labour Organization (ILO)
✦ United Nations Educational, Scientific and Cultural Organization (UNESCO).

NATO

✦ NATO is an intergovernmental military defence alliance.
✦ It was established in 1949.
✦ It has its headquarters in Brussels, Belgium.

+ The organisation provides for a system of collective defence – if a member country is attacked, the other members will come to its defence.
+ There are currently 30 NATO member states. The most recent countries to seek membership are Finland and Sweden. Besides European countries, its membership includes the USA, Canada and Turkey.
+ NATO also has a number of partnership arrangements with other countries and organisations from the Atlantic to Central Asia and cooperates with a network of international organisations.
+ While NATO has not been called upon to use its members' armed forces to defend their members' borders, it did take command of the UN-mandated International Security Assistance Force (ISAF) in Afghanistan in August 2003. Its mission was to enable the Afghan government to provide effective security across the country and to ensure that it would never again be a safe haven for terrorists. Its mission was completed at the end of 2014.
+ NATO has set a target for member countries to spend 2 per cent of their GDP on defence.
+ Following the 2017 general election, the new Conservative government pledged to maintain UK defence spending at the 2 per cent target figure set by NATO for the next ten years.
+ NATO is now also focused on the worldwide fight against terrorism and working to counter cyber terrorism.

The UK's role in NATO
+ The UK was a founding member of NATO.
+ It is the second largest contributor – financially and militarily – to NATO after the USA.

> **Case study**
>
> **The Russian invasion of Ukraine, 2022**
>
> Ukraine is not a member of NATO but it borders countries that are members. Prior to Russia's invasion of Ukraine, NATO countries were providing training to the Ukrainian armed forces.
>
> NATO member countries are now providing Ukraine with military and humanitarian assistance. Both Finland and Sweden are currently in the process of applying to join NATO as a result of the Russian invasion of Ukraine.
>
> If Russia did attack a NATO member country the other members of NATO are required to provide military assistance.

The European Union
Since this specification was approved, the UK has left the European Union (EU).
+ The EU was formerly known as the European Economic Community (EEC) and more usually as the Common Market.
+ The six founding member states who signed the Treaty of Rome in 1957 were France, West Germany, Belgium, The Netherlands, Luxembourg and Italy.
+ The Community aimed to encourage trade between member states, allow for the free of movement of people between member states and work towards 'an ever-closer union'.
+ The European Parliament divides its time between Brussels in Belgium and Strasbourg in France.
+ The decision-making process within the EU is different from that which operates in member states. Proposals for new laws, directives or initiatives are drafted by the European Commission. These are then considered by the member state governments at the Council of the European Union meetings. The European Parliament is then consulted.
+ Four times a year, heads of government from all the member states meet at the European Council to discuss the political direction and priorities of the EU.

Brexit, the UK's membership of the EU and its impact upon the UK

+ The UK did not join the EEC until 1973.
+ A referendum was held about the UK's membership of the EU in 1976 – two-thirds voted to remain in the EU.
+ As the EU sought to become more centralised (federal), for example, by creating a common currency (the euro), some UK politicians believed that the UK should leave the EU.
+ In 2016 a UK referendum was held and the people voted to leave the EU (commonly known as 'Brexit').
+ The UK has since renegotiated various trade and other agreements with the EU. The UK formally ceased to be an EU member state in January 2020.
+ At the time of writing, there is a dispute about the single market borders in Northern Ireland, which borders the Republic of Ireland (an EU member state).

Case study

The EU In–Out Referendum: the UK votes to leave the EU

Following the 2015 general election, the re-elected prime minister David Cameron reiterated a Conservative Party manifesto commitment to hold an 'In–Out' referendum on Britain's membership of the EU by the end of 2017, following renegotiations with EU leaders.

All the major political parties, with the exception of UKIP, supported the Remain vote. However, the issue cut across party political lines and there were supporters for both sides within each party.

While the television channels have to be politically neutral, the press was divided over the UK's membership. The *Daily Telegraph* supported a Leave vote while the *Daily Mirror*, *The Times*, the *Guardian* and the *Financial Times* supported a Remain vote.

The Remain campaign was led by the prime minister, David Cameron, and the chancellor of the exchequer, George Osborne.

Two of the leading Leave campaigners were also important members of the Conservative Party: Boris Johnson and the justice minister, Michael Gove.

The referendum took place on 23 June 2016.

The referendum result

+ Votes to Leave: 17,410,742 (51.9%)
+ Votes to Remain: 16,141,241 (48.1%)
+ The turnout was 72%.
+ The result showed some interesting voting patterns: in England, every counting region with the exception of London voted by a majority to Leave the EU.

Arguments for EU membership

Remain campaigners who supported UK membership of the EU pointed out the economic benefits to the UK of the UK's membership.
+ The Single Market with its 500 million people generates about £10 trillion of economic activity.
+ The EU accounts for half of the UK's overall trade and investments.
+ Around 3.5 million jobs in the UK are linked to its trade with the EU.

Arguments against EU membership

Leave campaigners believed that the EU was undermining the power of the UK Parliament to make decisions about life in the UK.
+ Many believed that the EU was an undemocratic body.
+ Their slogan of 'Take back control' encapsulated their campaign.

Table 12.1 shows the results of the 2016 Brexit referendum broken down by nation.

Table 12.1 The results of the 2016 EU referendum by nation

Nation	Vote to Leave (%)	Vote to Remain (%)	Turnout (%)
England	53.4	46.6	73.0
Scotland	38.0	62.0	67.2
Wales	52.5	47.5	71.7
Northern Ireland	44.2	55.8	62.9

Tip

Since the UK has now left the EU your revision on this topic should focus on the ongoing relationship and issues that have arisen since Brexit. Questions could focus on the benefits or otherwise of the UK's past membership compared to the nature of a post-Brexit UK (see the box at the top of the following page).

Post-Brexit

An example of an issue that has arisen post-Brexit concerns UK goods entering Northern Ireland. The goods have to be EU-checked before they enter Northern Ireland in case they enter the Republic of Ireland, which is an EU member state. This means that there is a customs barrier to free trade within the UK – in the North Sea. Many in Northern Ireland feel this is a barrier to trade in Northern Ireland.

The Council of Europe

+ The Council of Europe is the continent's leading human rights organisation.
+ 47 countries are members, of which 27 are also members of the EU.
+ The Council of Europe is not a part of the EU, but all EU member countries have agreed to abide by the European Convention on Human Rights.
+ The European Court of Human Rights (ECHR) oversees the implementation of the Convention.
+ The ECHR is made up of judges from all of the countries who are members of the Council of Europe.
+ Individual citizens can bring complaints of human rights violations to the Strasbourg Court, once all possibilities of appeal have been exhausted in their own country.
+ The EU is preparing to sign up to the European Convention on Human Rights, creating the ability for any of the 447 million citizens within the EU to access its articles of freedom.

The UK's role in the Council of Europe

+ The UK was a founder member of the Council of Europe.
+ UK legal experts played a major part in drafting the European Convention on Human Rights and in 1998 incorporated the Convention into UK law via the Human Rights Act (HRA).
+ In recent years, some UK politicians have stated that the UK should have its own Human Rights Bill rather than having adopted the Convention.

The European Convention on Human Rights

The Convention enshrines the basic human rights and fundamental freedoms of everyone within the jurisdiction of any member state. These include the right:
+ to life
+ to protection against torture and inhuman treatment
+ to freedom and safety
+ to a fair trial
+ to respect for private and family life
+ to freedom of expression (including freedom of the press), thought, conscience and religion
+ to freedom of peaceful assembly and association.

Tip

Make sure you don't confuse the Council of Europe with the European Union. The Council of Europe is responsible for the European Convention on Human Rights and hears cases in Strasbourg at the European Court of Human Rights. The court of the EU is called the Court of Justice of the European Union.

The Commonwealth

+ The Commonwealth developed after the Second World War as countries of the former British Empire gained their independence. Some retained the British monarch as head of state, others became republics.
+ Many Commonwealth countries had trade, aid and cultural links with the UK that they wished to retain.
+ The Commonwealth is a voluntary political association of member states.
+ Formerly known as the British Commonwealth, the Commonwealth has 2.5 billion citizens in 56 member countries, which span Africa, Asia, the Americas, Europe and the Pacific.
+ 32 of the members are small states with fewer than 1.5 million people.

Check your understanding and progress at **www.hoddereducation.co.uk/myrevisionnotes**

- It represents about 30 per cent of the world's population. Its members include some of the richest and some of the poorest countries in the world.
- All members must agree with the values set out in the Commonwealth Charter – democracy, human rights and the rule of law.
- The head of the Commonwealth is King Charles III.
- Its headquarters are in London, UK.
- Heads of government of the member states meet every two years at the Commonwealth Heads of Government Meeting (CHOGM).

The WTO

- The WTO came into being in 1955 as the successor body to the General Agreement on Tariffs and Trade (GATT), which was set up at the end of the Second World War.
- The UK was a member of GATT from 1948 and joined the WTO in 1955. It regained its place as a member when it left the EU.
- The WTO has 164 member countries and its headquarters are in Geneva, Switzerland.
- The WTO is the only global organisation dealing with trading rules between nations.
- The WTO claims to:
  - cut living costs and raise living standards
  - settle trade disputes and reduce trade tensions between nations
  - encourage economic growth and employment
  - cut the cost of doing business
  - encourage good governance
  - help countries develop
  - give the weak a stronger voice
  - help support health and the environment
  - contribute to peace and stability.

In regard to all the organisations covered in this section, with the exception of the EU, the UK was a founding member and has played a key role in their development and in their ongoing work.

The UK's role in solving international disputes

REVISED

- The UK has played an active part in attempting to resolve international disputes and conflicts.
- The methods used have varied and include mediation, humanitarian aid, sanctions and the use of force.
- Some of these interventions have been controversial and still divide public opinion.
- The Iraq Inquiry (also known as the Chilcot Inquiry, or Chilcot report, after its chairman, Sir John Chilcot) was set up in 2009 to investigate the UK's intervention in Iraq between 2001 and 2009 and the role of British troops in the Iraq War.

Mediation

- Mediation is a process involving outsiders in a dialogue to try to resolve disputes.
- The UK has been involved in numerous mediation attempts to resolve disputes and conflicts by seeking a peaceful resolution or sponsoring international conferences that lead to a peaceful resolution.

Mediation in Northern Ireland

The period from 1968 to 1998 in Northern Ireland is known as 'the Troubles'. Several attempts to seek a peaceful solution to the civil unrest and conflict between the opposing Unionist and Nationalist communities failed. The UK government imposed direct rule from Westminster. The bombing and killing then spread from Northern Ireland to the UK mainland.

By 1993, a framework had been set up to bring about an end to the Troubles, based upon the idea of 'consent': that any agreement could only proceed if the people of Northern Ireland consented to it. In 1996, former US Senator George Mitchell agreed to chair the Northern Ireland peace talks. After all-party talks, an agreement was announced on Good Friday 1998.

The Good Friday Agreement was put to the people of both Northern Ireland and the Republic of Ireland in a referendum, and both voted in favour of the agreement, which is still in force today. In this case, it took the influence of an outside but interested party – the USA – to enable an agreement, which involved the UK government, the government of the Irish Republic and all political parties in Northern Ireland, to be reached.

Sanctions

In 2022, over 70 countries have arms embargoes, trade sanctions and other trade restrictions imposed on them by the UK. Sanctions can involve:

+ arms embargoes, trade control restrictions and defence export policies against countries and terrorist organisations
+ collective action carried out by international bodies such as the EU, NATO or the UN, for example, the EU has taken collective action against Russia over its invasion of Ukraine in 2022
+ government sanctions against individuals
+ government-organised boycotts, for example, in February 2022, the UK and other governments refused to send official representatives to the Winter Olympics in China over human rights abuses there
+ boycotts organised and carried out by the public, for example, Nestlé, the Swiss-based company, faced a consumer boycott due to its aggressive marketing of baby milk formula, considered to be less heathy than breast milk, in Africa.

Use of force

+ The UK armed forces have been involved in numerous military actions since 1991 (see Table 12.2).
+ Most of the actions of British armed forces have involved working with others in alliances or in the allocation of troops to an international force under the control of an international body like the EU, NATO or the UN.
+ Many of these actions have proved to be controversial.
+ One parliamentary convention that has occurred since the Iraq War is that governments should obtain the approval of the House of Commons before committing British troops to action abroad.

Table 12.2 The use of UK forces abroad since 1991

Date	Event
1991	The Gulf War
1992–96	UN peacekeeping mission in the former Yugoslavia
1998	Operation Desert Fox – a four-day bombing campaign against targets in Iraq
1999	NATO-led campaigns in the former Republic of Yugoslavia and Kosovo
1999	East Timor, as part of a multinational peacekeeping force
2000	Sierra Leone, evacuating non-combatants and rescuing captured British troops
2001–14	Afghanistan – British troops were involved in combat operations as part of a US-led campaign
2003	EU-led crisis management in the Democratic Republic of Congo
2003	Invasion of Iraq – British troops remained in Iraq until 2011
2011	Military intervention in Libya
2014	Iraq and Syria – Operation Shader
2019	Persian Gulf Crisis

Check your understanding and progress at **www.hoddereducation.co.uk/myrevisionnotes**

House of Commons votes on military action since 2010

+ 9 September 2010: continued deployment of UK Armed Forces in Afghanistan (agreed 310 to 14)
+ 21 March 2011: (retrospective) approval for enforcement of no-fly-zone in Libya (agreed 557 to 13)
+ 29 August 2013: military action to alleviate humanitarian suffering in Syria (defeated 272 to 285)
+ 26 September 2014: use of UK air strikes to support Iraqi security forces' efforts against Islamic State in Iraq (agreed 524 to 43).

The work of non-governmental organisations

REVISED

+ Many non-governmental organisations (NGOs) are charities which provide services to those in need in their own country and overseas.
+ Many work alongside government bodies and they may receive government funding.
+ The Disasters Emergency Committee (DEC) works with a range of NGOs to provide urgent help and relief. DEC works with 13 leading UK aid charities in times of crisis. Since its launch in 1963, it has run 75 appeals and raised more than £1.7 billion.
+ The UK government was the first country in the G7 to honour the UN target set in 1970 of ring-fencing 0.7 per cent of its gross national income (GNI) for international aid spending.
+ The work of NGOs is best examined through specific case studies. The websites of several NGOs are provided in the useful websites box below.

Useful websites

These are the official websites of the organisations named in this chapter:
+ The Commonwealth: **www.thecommonwealth.org**
+ Council of Europe: **www.coe.int/en**
+ European Union: **www.europa.eu/index_en.htm**
+ NATO: **www.nato.int**
+ United Nations: **www.un.org/en**
+ UN non-governmental organisations: **http://en.unesco.org/partnerships/non-governmental-organizations/list**
+ World Trade Organization: **www.wto.org**

Examples of non-governmental organisations concerned with humanitarian aid:
+ Action Against Hunger: **www.actionagainsthunger.org/**
+ CARE: **www.care.org/**
+ Doctors Without Borders/Medecins Sans Frontieres: **https://msf.org.uk/**
+ International Federation of the Red Cross and Red Crescent Societies: **www.ifrc.org/**
+ Oxfam International: **www.oxfam.org/en**
+ Refugees International: **www.refugeesinternational.org/**

An article about the UK government cutting overseas aid:
+ BBC News: **www.bbc.co.uk/news/57362816**

Key points check

Can you answer the key points related to this chapter? If you are unclear about how to respond to any of these questions, revisit the relevant topics in the chapter.

+ What is the role of the UK within:
    + the UN
    + NATO
    + the Council of Europe
    + the WTO
    + the Commonwealth?
+ What is the relationship between the UK and the EU?
+ How are international disputes and conflicts resolved?
+ What is the role and work of NGOs?

Now test yourself (AO1)

TESTED

1 Identify one form of sanction.

2 Identity the reason why NATO was established.

3 Define what is meant by 'soft power'.

4 Explain why the UK has a veto on decisions at the UN.

5 Name the body that drafts policy ideas within the EU.

Exam practice

Source A: Russia's invasion of Ukraine

In 2014, Russia invaded Ukraine and has since occupied some parts of the country closest to Russia.

Then, in February 2022, Russia launched a full-scale invasion of Ukraine. The invasion has led to a full-scale war in Ukraine, leading to millions of people being displaced and leaving the economy in ruins.

1 Discuss two possible forms of intervention the UK could take that might make Russia reconsider its position. [4] (AO2)

2 Examine the benefits to the UK of leaving the EU. [8] (AO3)

3* The UK government has temporarily cut its spending on overseas aid. Evaluate the case made by those who say we should spend more on aid and those who state we should spend the money on public services.

In your answer you should consider:
+ how the UK overseas aid budget is spent
+ UK public services and how they are funded. [8] (AO3)

Remember, the * means this is a synoptic question, which draws upon your knowledge and understanding from more than one theme. You can find more information on page 10.

Check your understanding and progress at **www.hoddereducation.co.uk/myrevisionnotes**

13 What laws does a society require and why? (3.3.1)

Remember, the first section of each of the three themes outlines the major concepts of that theme and introduces elements that are followed up in greater depth later in the section.

The fundamental principles of law

The system of law used in the UK is based upon several key concepts that revolve around the key idea of the 'rule of law':

> Every person, no matter who they are, is subject to the law, and every person should be treated equally.

This concept incorporates the principles described in Table 13.1.

Table 13.1 The principles of the 'rule of law'

Key principle	Definition	Comments
The idea of legal certainty	All laws in the UK must be applied in a precise and predictable manner.	Citizens must believe that the law is fair, predictable and transparent. If they do they are more likely to obey it.
That laws are properly enacted and clear in their purpose	Laws are formally agreed and the purpose of any law is clearly set out.	It is important that laws are enacted by due process. Laws should be clear in their intention.
That there is equality and **fairness** in the law	Every person should be allowed equal access to the justice system. Fairness relates to treating people equally, for example, two people from differing circumstances who each commit the same offence for the first time should not be dealt with differently.	The law applies to every individual in society equally – even members of the royal family have appeared in court and been convicted. The legal system should treat everyone equally and not provide unfair access to the law to anyone. Those charged and found guilty of an offence should not be treated differently.
That laws cannot be retrospective	Legislation cannot be pre-dated. You cannot be tried for an action that was not unlawful at the time.	Provides citizens with certainty about the law.
That there is due legal process	The judicial system must operate as laid down in law. Certain rights are guaranteed: + a fair trial + the right to defend oneself + the right to be represented + if found guilty, the right of appeal.	This is an important guarantee of a citizen's rights and is fundamental to the operation of our justice system.

> **Tip**
>
> There is no requirement to know the specific wording of these principles, but you need to be able to show you understand them and how they are interconnected.

There is also a range of other concepts, terms and expressions that relate to the way the UK's justice system operates.

Table 13.2 outlines some other building blocks of the UK's legal system, which have developed as a result of the nature of 'the rule of law'.

Table 13.2 The fundamental principles of law

Term	Definition	Comments
Justice	This is a concept based upon our behaviour or treatment relating to what is morally right and fair. There are differences of opinion between various countries and societies about what justice entails. Each country's justice system is based upon a system of moral values, which can differ from one country to another.	This is an overarching concept that underpins our understanding of the legal and judicial process. It relates to ideas such as fairness, equality and due process.
Presumption of innocence	Within the UK's legal system a person who is brought before a court is presumed innocent. The state has to prove the person's guilt beyond reasonable doubt. The accused does not have to prove their innocence.	This is a basic principle within our legal system. Some judicial systems assume guilt and it is up to the accused to prove their innocence.
Trial by jury	An early principle of English justice was that people accused of a crime should be judged by their 'peers', i.e. people of equal standing from their community. A jury hears the evidence and following a summing up by the judge determines guilt or innocence. In England, Wales and Northern Ireland there are 12 members of a jury. In Scotland there are 15.	In recent years the idea of a majority verdict has been introduced to avoid any attempt to bribe or threaten any jury member. A judge can, if asked, allow for a majority vote of at most ten to two. Normally a jury must reach a decision on which all 12 members agree.
Access to justice	This principle relates to the ability of any individual citizen to be able to access and use the justice system irrespective of their status or wealth within society.	Many argue that in general terms the UK system upholds this principle. Others state that the many changes made regarding legal aid, especially in regard to civil law cases, mean access to the law can be dependent upon one's wealth.

An overview of the nature of the UK's justice system

> The purpose of the criminal justice system is to deliver justice for all, by convicting and punishing the guilty and helping them to stop offending, while protecting the innocent. It is responsible for detecting crime and bringing it to justice; and carrying out the orders of court, such as collecting fines, and supervising community and custodial punishment.

Source: an extract from a presentation by Jon Collins, campaign director of the Criminal Justice Alliance, to the Centre for Parliamentary Studies, 18 May 2010.

Citizen involvement in the judicial process

Within a democracy, judicial processes are ultimately based upon the consent of the people. This is reinforced in the UK by the involvement of ordinary citizens in the operation and decision-making processes within the justice system.

+ Members of a jury: randomly selected citizens determine the outcome in many trials. This role is seen as a very important citizenship duty.

Check your understanding and progress at **www.hoddereducation.co.uk/myrevisionnotes**

- Magistrates: ordinary citizens can volunteer to serve as magistrates (Justices of the Peace – JPs). Magistrates determine most minor criminal cases in the Magistrates' Courts.
- Special constables: volunteers who support the work of full-time police officers.
- Police and crime commissioners: publicly elected officials who are responsible for the strategy and budget of a local police force.

How rules and laws are used to deal with injustice and discrimination

REVISED

Figure 13.1 illustrates how rules and laws operate in the UK legal system.

The term 'rules' relates to the way a group or organisation operates.

The term 'laws' relates to the way in which society is regulated.

Rules and laws are made in society to help us to deal with complex problems of fairness, justice and discrimination. Discrimination relates to people being treated differently based on their age, sexuality, ethnicity or disability.

In recent years legislation has been passed making unfairness, injustice and discrimination unlawful and punishable by the courts.

Rules example:
Muirfield Golf Club was banned from holding the Open Championship because it did not allow female members. After a second vote a majority of members voted in favour of changing its membership rules.

Recent anti-discrimination legislation passed in the UK:
- Race Relations Acts 1965, 1968, 1976 and 2000
- Equal Pay Act 1970
- Sex Discrimination Acts 1975 and 2002
- Disability Discrimination Acts 1995 and 2005
- Equality Acts 2006 and 2010

Figure 13.1 Rules and laws

> **Tip**
>
> There is no requirement to know the specific dates and nature of each piece of anti-discrimination legislation. The important Act to know about is the Equality Act 2010, which merged all the previous equality legislation into the new Act and created what is now the Equality and Human Rights Commission, which has responsibility for enforcing the legislation.

Rights and responsibilities in local and global situations

REVISED

- Different societies, cultures and countries have different views on some legal issues. For example, the death penalty was abolished in the UK but is still used in other countries such as the USA.

+ Legislation can change when different governments take power, or when situations change. For example, during the Covid-19 pandemic the government was forced to introduce some measures that had an impact on people's rights.

The Universal Declaration of Human Rights

+ When the Second World War ended in 1945, the United Nations (UN) was set up. The UN established an agreement on human rights that exist for all people.
+ The Universal Declaration of Human Rights (UDHR) was proclaimed in 1948. It was added to in 1976 and became international law.
+ 192 countries are currently signed up to some or all of the UDHR.

The European Convention on Human Rights

+ After the UDHR was proclaimed, the Council of Europe devised the European Convention on Human Rights in 1950.
+ The UK played a major role in drafting the Convention and was one of the original signatories.
+ In 1998, the UK wrote the Convention into UK law via the Human Rights Act (HRA). Many other member countries have done the same.

Rights v. responsibilities

+ There has to be a balance struck between the power of the state and the rights and duties of its citizens. At times, this balance is brought into question (see first box).
+ Many citizens make use of the European Court of Human Rights in Strasbourg when they are in a human rights dispute with authorities in their own countries (see second box).

Rights v. responsibilities examples

+ In the UK the police have powers of 'stop and search', but many citizens from minority ethnic groups argue that they are subject to the use of these powers more than other groups. This eventually led to the government changing the guidance on the use of stop and search.
+ In March 2020 during the Covid-19 pandemic the government decided there would be a total lockdown of society. During this time, the government controlled what citizens could do and when.

Russia and the European Court of Human Rights

+ In 2017, the European Court of Human Rights (ECHR) ruled in favour of a group of Russian citizens regarding how the Russian government and it forces ended a siege at a school in Beslan when terrorists had taken 1,000 hostages. A total of 330 civilians, many of them children, died as a result of Russian armed forces storming the building. The ECHR found that the Russian government had not taken sufficient precautions based on prior information about the terrorists and that it used undue force to end the situation. The Russian government said that the ruling was 'utterly unacceptable' and that it would appeal.
+ Following the invasion of Ukraine by Russian armed forces, Russian membership of the Council of Europe was suspended in March 2022.

Tip

This is a topic where it is very helpful to have studied a case study from which you can quote, so that you can demonstrate both knowledge and understanding of the topic.

Useful websites

Equality and Human Rights Commission: **www.equalityhumanrights.com**

European Convention on Human Rights – a full copy of the Convention in English: **www.echr.coe.int/Documents/Convention_ENG.pdf**

European Court of Human Rights: **www.coe.int/t/democracy/migration/bodies/echr_en.asp**

Universal Declaration of Human Rights: **www.un.org/en/universal-declaration-human-rights**

Key points check

Can you answer the key points related to this chapter? If you are unclear about how to respond to any of these questions, revisit the relevant topics in the chapter.
+ What are the basic principles of law?
+ What do you understand by the terms 'justice' and 'fairness'?
+ What laws has the UK introduced to outlaw discrimination?
+ Why is the Universal Declaration of Human Rights (UDHR) important?

Now test yourself (AO1)   TESTED

1 Identify which of the following Acts of Parliament linked all existing anti-discrimination legislation together:
   a Race Relations Act
   b Disability Discrimination Act
   c Equality Act
   d Equal Pay Act
2 What is meant by the term 'discrimination'?
3 Name the body that is responsible for the Universal Declaration of Human Rights (UDHR).
4 Explain how a rule differs from a law.
5 Identify one way citizens in the UK can take part in the judicial process.
6 Define what is meant by the expression 'the rule of law'.

Exam practice

Source A: the presumption of guilt

> Being presumed guilty is frustrating, burdensome and exhausting. In the criminal justice system it can also be dangerous and life threatening. When police, prosecutors or judges presume someone's guilt, lives are destroyed and horrific injustices take place. We need to talk about this problem in the United States.
>
> Source: **www.huffingtonpost.com/bryan-stevenson/tremaine-mcmillian-case_b_3560827.html**

1 Describe how the justice system in the UK takes a different view than that indicated in Source A. [4] (AO2)
2 Examine the view that a citizen has both rights and responsibilities within society. [8] (AO3)
3* Evaluate the arguments made in favour of the media being able to fully report on all court cases taking place in the UK.

In your answer you should consider:
+ the current ability of the media to report court cases
+ the nature of different types of court cases heard in the UK. [8] (AO3)

Remember, the * means this is a synoptic question, which draws upon your knowledge and understanding from more than one theme. You can find more information on page 10.

The operation of the justice system

The justice system has five parts:
+ the police
+ the judiciary
+ legal representatives
+ criminal and civil law courts
+ tribunals and dispute resolution.

The role of the police

The role and responsibilities of the police as laid down in the police service's Statement of Common Purpose is as follows:
+ The purpose of the police service is to uphold the law fairly and firmly.
+ To prevent crime; to pursue and bring to justice those who break the law.
+ To keep the King's peace.
+ To protect, help and reassure the community.
+ To be seen to do this with integrity, common sense and sound judgement.

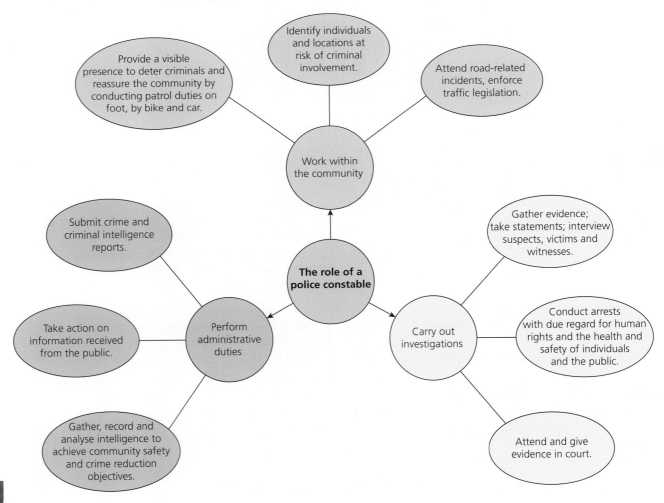

Figure 14.1 The role of a police constable

Check your understanding and progress at **www.hoddereducation.co.uk/myrevisionnotes**

Another way of considering the role of the police is to consider the force's core operational duties, which include:

+ protecting life and property
+ preserving order
+ preventing the commission of offences (crime prevention)
+ bringing offenders to justice.

The police have other additional duties that are laid down under legislation and common law. The role of a police constable is illustrated in Figure 14.1.

Tip

There is no requirement to recall all of the different jobs performed by the police, but you should have an understanding of the range of work the police undertake.

The powers of the police

Table 14.1 summarises the powers most commonly used by UK police.

Table 14.1 The powers most commonly used by the police in the UK

Police power	Commentary
Stop and search	A police officer has powers to stop and search if they have 'reasonable grounds' to suspect someone is carrying: + illegal drugs + a weapon + stolen property + something which could be used to commit a crime.
Power of arrest	To arrest someone the police need reasonable grounds to suspect the person has been involved in a crime for which an arrest is necessary. The police have powers to arrest anywhere and at any time, including on the street, at home or at a workplace. When carrying out an arrest the police must tell the suspect why they are being arrested.
Entry, search and seizure	In certain circumstances set out in the Police and Criminal Evidence Act 1984 (PACE), the police have the power to enter premises and search them to either arrest someone or seize items in connection with a crime, or both. Police usually need to obtain a warrant from the court before they can enter and search premises. The police may seize anything which is on a premises if they have reasonable grounds for believing it has been used to commit an offence.

From a citizenship perspective it is also important to understand that:

+ the UK doesn't have a national police force
+ the police service is operated on a regional basis
+ the aim is that the police should have local accountability
+ there are 43 distinct police forces in the UK – Scotland and Northern Ireland each have a single police force
+ the Metropolitan police force in London does provide some national services to the other police forces
+ today, each police force in England and Wales has a directly elected police and crime commissioner, with the exception of the two London-based forces
+ within each police force the day-to-day operations are the responsibility of the chief constable, who is accountable to their police and crime commissioner
+ in London the mayor shares police oversight with the home secretary.

The role of the judiciary

The role of the judiciary is to:

+ administer justice according to the law
+ pass sentences in criminal cases
+ make decisions in civil law cases.

Table 14.2 summarises the different roles of the members of the judiciary in the UK.

Except for magistrates, the other members of the judiciary listed are professionally trained lawyers and most of the posts outlined are full time and salaried.

Table 14.2 The different roles within the hierarchy of the judiciary

Role	Responsibilities
Lord Chief Justice	The most senior judge in the UK: the head of an independent judiciary
President of the Supreme Court	Head of the UK's highest domestic appeal court
Justices of the Supreme Court	Judges who hear civil and criminal appeals in the UK's most senior court
Senior President of Tribunals	The head of the judges in the UK Tribunal Service
Master of the Rolls	President of the Court of Appeal (Civil Division)
Chancellor of the High Court	The head of the Chancery Division of the High Court
President of the Family Division	Head of Family Justice
President of the King's Bench Division	Also the Deputy Head of Criminal Justice
Lord Justices of Appeal	These judges hear appeal cases in the civil and criminal divisions of the Court of Appeal
High Court Judges	These judges may hear trial and appeal cases in the High Court, sit on some appeals in the Court of Appeal and judge serious cases in Crown Court trials
Circuit judges	These judges hear criminal cases in Crown Courts and civil cases in the County Courts
Recorders	These judges work part time hearing criminal cases in the Crown Court and civil cases in County Courts; they are qualified **barristers** or **solicitors**
District judge	These judges hear the bulk of civil cases in the County Courts
District judge (Magistrates' Court)	These judges deal with the most complex cases in a Magistrates' Court
Tribunal judges	These judges deal with most cases brought before tribunal hearings; they often sit with lay members
Magistrates	Magistrates are volunteers from the local communities who agree to sit and dispense justice in Magistrates' Courts. They are also referred to as Justices of the Peace (JPs). They receive training and are supported by legal advice in the courtroom. They normally sit as a 'bench' of three magistrates. In 2022, there were 12,561 magistrates, compared with 22,214 in 2014.

Table 14.3 summarises the role of judges in the UK judicial system.

Table 14.3 The role of judges

Role	Responsibilities
Preside over court proceedings	Judges ensure that a court case follows agreed rules.
	They also provide advice on points of law and give guidance to a jury on the evidence and points of law.
Interpret and apply the law	Judges have to interpret the law as drafted by parliament and apply it to the case under consideration.
Create case law	Where the law is unclear, judges have to make rulings.
	Once these are upheld or used by other courts they become judge-created 'case law'.
Decide sentencing	Judges determines the sentence following a jury decision.
	The amount of discretion a judge has regarding the sentence is now limited as sentencing policy is often laid down by law.
Chair public inquiries and commissions	Judges undertake this role because they are seen as independent and impartial.
	Inquiries are organised and run along the lines of a court hearing.
	The Covid-19 inquiry into the pandemic – set up in 2022 and expected to start taking evidence in 2023 – is a judge-led inquiry.
Protect the citizen from an overbearing state	If a citizen has a grievance about the power of the state the judiciary is an independent body that can adjudicate.

Check your understanding and progress at **www.hoddereducation.co.uk/myrevisionnotes**

Powers of the judiciary

Judges play many roles and have a range of powers:

+ They have the power to interpret the law.
+ They have the power to control hearings and trials in their courtrooms.
+ Most important of all, following a decision by a jury they alone have the power to determine the sentence given, often within published sentencing guidelines.
+ Increasingly the range of sentences for specific offences is laid down within legislation so judges have limited room for manoeuvre.
+ In the statements they make in court, judges do have the power to influence debate and discussion on specific topics.
+ In almost all civil cases judges sit without a jury so determine the merits of the evidence and decide the outcome of the cases and any award made.

The roles of legal representatives

The three main branches of the legal profession are:

+ legal executives
+ solicitors
+ barristers.

Tip

A way of recalling the roles of legal representatives is to equate them to health:

+ the legal executive is the paramedic
+ the solicitor is the family doctor
+ the barrister is the hospital consultant.

If they have a civil dispute, many people, especially those with limited means, visit their local Citizens Advice office to seek free legal advice.

How the different criminal and civil courts work

Figure 14.2 indicates that the criminal and civil court system is interlinked.

+ Magistrates and Crown Courts deal mainly with criminal cases.
+ County and Family Courts deal with civil cases.

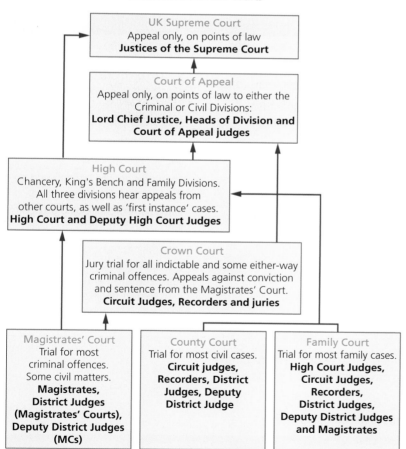

The Structure of the Courts

UK Supreme Court
Appeal only, on points of law
Justices of the Supreme Court

Court of Appeal
Appeal only, on points of law to either the Criminal or Civil Divisions:
Lord Chief Justice, Heads of Division and Court of Appeal judges

High Court
Chancery, King's Bench and Family Divisions. All three divisions hear appeals from other courts, as well as 'first instance' cases.
High Court and Deputy High Court Judges

Crown Court
Jury trial for all indictable and some either-way criminal offences. Appeals against conviction and sentence from the Magistrates' Court.
Circuit Judges, Recorders and juries

Magistrates' Court
Trial for most criminal offences. Some civil matters.
Magistrates, District Judges (Magistrates' Courts), Deputy District Judges (MCs)

County Court
Trial for most civil cases.
Circuit judges, Recorders, District Judges, Deputy District Judge

Family Court
Trial for most family cases.
High Court Judges, Circuit Judges, Recorders, District Judges, Deputy District Judges and Magistrates

Figure 14.2 The court structure in England and Wales

Table 14.4 illustrates how the progress of criminal and civil cases through the courts differs.

Table 14.4 Differences between criminal and civil processes

Element of the process	Criminal Courts	Civil Courts
Court case	The Crown Prosecution Service decides whether a case is brought on behalf of the state.	The case, or claim, is brought by an individual, group or organisation.
Decision	The defendant is convicted if guilty or acquitted if not guilty. The decision is made by a jury or magistrates.	The defendant is found liable or not liable (responsible) in regard to the issue.
Level of proof required	Beyond reasonable doubt.	Preponderance of evidence. Evidence must be produced to support the claim.
Burden of proof	The accused is innocent until proven guilty. The prosecution must prove their case; the accused does not have to prove their innocence.	The claimant must give proof of the claim.
Sanctions	**Non-custodial** or custodial sentence given if found guilty.	Compensation awarded or an injunction (an order to stop taking an action) granted.
Appeal	The defendant may appeal a court's verdict in regard to either the verdict or the sentence. It is now possible for the state to ask for the sentence to be reviewed.	Either party can appeal a court's decision.

Tribunals and other means of dispute resolution

Table 14.5 covers the key points about the work of tribunals and ombudsmen.

Table 14.5 Tribunals and ombudsmen

	Details	Advantages	Disadvantages
Tribunals	Tribunals are inferior courts. They deal with a large number of cases each year. A variety of subjects are dealt with by specialised tribunals. These include employment, health and social care, pensions and finance, and commerce.	Can deal with specialised issues. Simple and informal procedure. Can be cheaper than conventional courts. Can be quicker than the court system.	Applicants who pay legal professionals to represent them tend to be more successful, which possibly results in inequality for those who cannot afford this option. Reasons for decisions reached are not always clear.
Ombudsmen	An ombudsman is an official who is appointed to check on government activity on behalf of an individual citizen and to investigate complaints that are made. This can be in a range of areas, e.g. health service, local government, legal services and housing. Ombudsmen also operate within the private sector.	The problem may be solved. Can lead to recommended changes made to government agencies or public bodies.	Their powers are constrained by the fact that they cannot deal with matters that could be dealt with by the courts. Complaints must be made through an elected representative and so this can be a barrier to citizens wishing to scrutinise government actions.

In recent years the government has encouraged the use of a system called Alternative Dispute Resolution (ADR) to help citizens resolve legal issues (see Table 14.6).

Table 14.6 Different methods of Alternative Dispute Resolution (ADR)

Type of ADR	Advantages	Disadvantages
Negotiation Parties involved discuss issues and compromise or make a decision about how the issues can be resolved.	Very informal. No cost. Private.	The parties involved may not be able to make a decision or compromise.

Check your understanding and progress at **www.hoddereducation.co.uk/myrevisionnotes**

Table 14.6 *continued*

Type of ADR	Advantages	Disadvantages
Mediation Parties discuss disputes with a neutral third party known as a mediator. The mediator does not disclose their own opinion but instead acts as a facilitator who helps the parties reach their own agreement.	Much cheaper than courts. Parties reach their own agreement, so likely to last longer than settlements that are forced on them.	The process may not lead to a settlement. The process is not binding.
Conciliation A conciliator is used to help to resolve disputes but plays a more active role than a mediator, e.g. they might suggest grounds for a possible compromise.	It is much cheaper than other forms of legal action. It is entirely private. It has a good success rate.	Process may not lead to a settlement and so parties may have to litigate anyway. Can put pressure on claimants to settle in employment cases and mean that they might accept a lesser settlement than a tribunal would award.
Arbitration The process whereby parties agree to have their dispute heard by a private arbitrator who will make a binding decision.	Can be cheaper than courts. Decisions are binding and can be enforced by courts. Parties can choose their own arbitrator. Quicker than court proceedings.	No state funding for arbitration. Professional arbitrators' fees can be high, so may be as expensive as courts. Using professional arbitrators and lawyers might cause delays similar to those experienced in the court system.

> **Tip**
>
> The term 'role' often appears in the specification and in exam questions. It is a shorthand phrase for stating the position, purpose or function of someone or something in a situation, organisation or society.

Rights and legal entitlements of citizens at differing ages

REVISED

Table 14.7 shows some of the more important rights acquired at various ages:
+ Historically, 21 was seen as the age when a person reached adulthood and acquired full legal rights.
+ In recent decades young people have acquired more rights at earlier ages, for example the right to vote at 18 (it had previously been 21).
+ In Scotland and Wales the voting age was lowered to 16 for local councils and the national parliaments (in the UK, the voting age for general elections is still 18).
+ The three major stepping stones for rights now occur at ages 16, 18 and 21 (see Table 14.7).

Table 14.7 Some of the rights acquired at the ages of 16, 18 and 21

Age	Rights
16	You can work full time if you have left school, have a National Insurance number and the job has accredited training. You can give consent and have sex. You can be married or live together with a parent's permission. You can be prosecuted for having sex with someone who is under 16. You can apply for your own passport with a parent's consent.
18	You have reached the age of majority (that is, you are an adult!). You can have a tattoo or body piercing. You can watch an 18 film and play an 18 computer game.

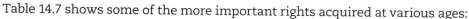

Table 14.7 *continued*

Age	Rights
	National minimum wage entitlement increases.
	You can get a cheque card and credit card.
	You can change your name.
	You can vote and be called for jury service.
	You can buy and drink alcohol in a bar. You can get married, enter a civil partnership or live together without parental consent.
	You can stand as an MP or a local councillor.
21	You can drive certain kinds of larger vehicles, like lorries or buses (with the appropriate licence).
	You are now entitled to full national minimum wage.
	You can apply to adopt a child.
	You can get certain types of jobs, e.g. become a driving instructor.
	You can apply for a licence to fly commercial transport, e.g. aeroplanes, helicopters, gyroplanes and airships.
	You can go into 21+ venues (some pubs, clubs and bars).

> **Tip**
>
> In your exam, focus on several rights from each of the key ages shown in Table 14.7 that indicate an increasing sense of gaining rights within society.

How civil law differs from criminal law

REVISED

It is helpful when revising this element of the course to refer back to the section earlier in this chapter, 'How the different criminal and civil courts work', pages 107–108.

+ Civil law deals with disputes between individuals such debt or divorce.
+ Criminal law deals with individuals and groups who are accused of breaking the law, for example, via theft, violence or rioting.

How the legal systems differ within the UK

REVISED

+ Due to the history of the UK there are three slightly differing legal systems in operation.
+ Within this book unless stated differently the text refers to legal practice in England and Wales.

The legal system in Northern Ireland

+ The UK Supreme Court hears all appeals on points of law in cases of major importance.
+ The Court of Appeal hears appeals on points of law in criminal and civil cases from all courts.
+ The High Court hears complex or important civil cases and appeals from County Courts.
+ County Courts hear a wide range of actions including Small Claims and family cases.
+ Magistrates' Courts (including Youth Courts and Family Proceedings) hear less serious criminal cases, cases involving juveniles, and civil and family cases.
+ Coroner's Courts investigate unexplained deaths.
+ The Enforcement of Judgments Office enforces civil judgments.

The legal system in Scotland

+ The Court of Session is the supreme civil court of Scotland. It is both a Trial Court and a Court of Appeal.
+ The High Court of Justiciary is the court that hears the most serious criminal cases. It also acts as an Appeal Court.

Check your understanding and progress at **www.hoddereducation.co.uk/myrevisionnotes**

✛ The Sheriff Appeal Court decides appeals against lower court decisions.

✛ Sheriff Court cases are heard by the sheriff and a jury of 15 jurors (members of the public). A sheriff may hear cases without a jury.

✛ The Justices of the Peace Court acts in a similar fashion to the Magistrates' Court system in England and Wales.

Useful websites

The Bar Council: **www.barcouncil.org.uk**

Chartered Institute of Legal Executives: **www.cilex.org.uk**

Courts and Tribunals Judiciary: **www.judiciary.gov.uk**

Crown Prosecution Service: **www.cps.gov.uk**

The Law Society: **www.lawsociety.org.uk**

nidirect government services: **www.nidirect.gov.uk/articles/introduction-justice-system**

Police.UK: **www.police.uk**

Scottish government: **www.gov.scot**

Key points check

Can you answer the key points related to this chapter? If you are unclear about how to respond to any of these questions, revisit the relevant topics in the chapter.

✛ What are the powers of the police?

✛ Why are judges important?

✛ How does criminal law differ from civil law?

✛ What are my rights at different ages?

✛ How does the legal system differ in different parts of the UK?

Now test yourself (AO1)

TESTED ◯

1 Identify a legal right given at the age of 18.

2 At what age can you vote in local elections in Wales and Scotland?

3 Explain the main role of the Crown Prosecution Service (CPS).

4 Define what is meant by 'case law'.

5 What are the names of the highest Courts of Appeal in Scotland?

Exam practice

Source A: requirements of law

A nine-year-old boy was arrested and charged with criminal damage and appeared without legal representation in a Magistrates' Court. The magistrates remanded the boy in custody and referred the case to the Crown Court.

1 Referencing the case in Source A, consider how it could be claimed not to conform to the requirements of the law in England. [4] (AO2)

2 Examine the case for or against there being one national police force in the UK. [8] (AO3)

3* In some countries members of the judiciary are directly elected by voters or appointed by political parties. Justify a case to argue that the UK is correct not to adopt this approach to appointing members of the judiciary.

In your answer you should consider:

✛ the current way in which members of the judiciary are appointed

✛ how the notion of political appointments conflicts with the principles underpinning the UK legal system. [8] (AO3)

Remember, the * means this is a synoptic question, which draws upon your knowledge and understanding from more than one theme. You can find more information on page 10.

111

How citizens' rights have changed and developed over time

Magna Carta

Figure 15.1 shows how the nature of the demand for rights has changed over time and, for some rights, is still changing.

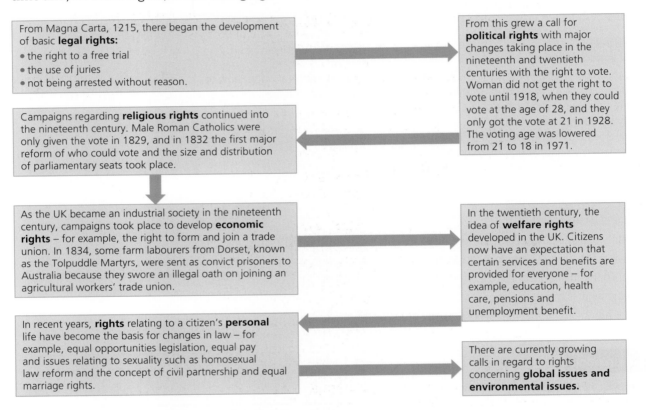

From Magna Carta, 1215, there began the development of basic **legal rights**:
- the right to a free trial
- the use of juries
- not being arrested without reason.

From this grew a call for **political rights** with major changes taking place in the nineteenth and twentieth centuries with the right to vote. Woman did not get the right to vote until 1918, when they could vote at the age of 28, and they only got the vote at 21 in 1928. The voting age was lowered from 21 to 18 in 1971.

Campaigns regarding **religious rights** continued into the nineteenth century. Male Roman Catholics were only given the vote in 1829, and in 1832 the first major reform of who could vote and the size and distribution of parliamentary seats took place.

As the UK became an industrial society in the nineteenth century, campaigns took place to develop **economic rights** – for example, the right to form and join a trade union. In 1834, some farm labourers from Dorset, known as the Tolpuddle Martyrs, were sent as convict prisoners to Australia because they swore an illegal oath on joining an agricultural workers' trade union.

In the twentieth century, the idea of **welfare rights** developed in the UK. Citizens now have an expectation that certain services and benefits are provided for everyone – for example, education, health care, pensions and unemployment benefit.

In recent years, **rights** relating to a citizen's **personal** life have become the basis for changes in law – for example, equal opportunities legislation, equal pay and issues relating to sexuality such as homosexual law reform and the concept of civil partnership and equal marriage rights.

There are currently growing calls in regard to rights concerning **global issues and environmental issues.**

Figure 15.1 How rights have developed since Magna Carta

Case study

The right to vote

+ Women only fully achieved the right to vote in 1928.
+ In 1968 the voting age was lowered to 18 from 21.
+ In 2014 the voting age for the Scottish independence referendum was lowered to 16.
+ In the 2019 general election some political parties campaigned for the voting age for all elections to be lowered to 16.
+ In Scotland and Wales, the voting age is now 16 for elections to local councils and their national parliaments.

Tip

There is no requirement to know the full details of Magna Carta (the Great Charter) of 1215, but you should understand how it challenged the concept of the king's power and authority at the time.

The Human Rights Act (HRA) 1998

+ This Act ensured that the European Convention on Human Rights was embedded in UK law.
+ It codified and combined all existing UK human rights legislation and while it did not extend existing human rights, it did ensure they were embraced within a single Act.
+ This meant that UK citizens could bring cases before UK courts and have them resolved without having to go to the European Court of Human Rights in Strasbourg.
+ It also meant that UK courts had to abide by and take account of decisions of the European Court of Human Rights when arriving at their decisions.

> **Tip**
>
> Do not confuse the European Convention on Human Rights and the European Court of Human Rights (ECHR) in Strasbourg with the European Union. They are two very different bodies. The Convention and ECHR are a part of the Council of Europe, which has nothing to do with the European Union.
>
> The European Union has its own court – the European Court of Justice (ECJ) – that meets in Luxembourg. It can be confusing because the European Union Parliament meets in Brussels and Strasbourg.

Common law and legislation

Table 15.1 introduces the features of common law and legislation.

Table 15.1 Common law and legislation features

Common law	Legislation	Comparison
Law that has developed as a result of rulings made by judges in court cases.	Also known as statute law, these are Acts of Parliament that set the will of parliament in regard to an area of life and may include the prescription of sanctions or punishments.	Common law has the ability to adjust with time and helps redefine laws that are unclear or are being interpreted for the first time. Lawyers refer to the latest ruling when preparing cases. Legislation or statute law is static until it is amended or superseded by a new law passed by parliament.

How the two types of law can operate

+ Parliament may pass a new Road Traffic Act that states that driving while under the influence of drugs is a criminal offence.
+ A person may be charged with this offence and their lawyer looks at any previous judgments to see if any aspect of the law has been clarified. For example, the issue may relate to a driver who is taking a combination of prescribed drugs.
+ If the law is unclear, the driver might challenge the charge and ask the judge to clarify the situation.
+ The judge's clarification then becomes case law that can be used by others in the future.
+ If the case progresses to higher courts, other judges can make fresh decisions that either dismiss the earlier case law or support it.
+ If parliament believes this case law undermines its original intention regarding the law it can change the law.

The right to representation

Representation in this context relates to how people join together in mutual support to achieve mutually agreed aims. This element of the course is only concerned with the role of trade unions and employer associations.

Trade unions

+ Trade unions were created to represent groups of workers who are their members.
+ They engage in negotiations with employers on issues such as wages, safety concerns, redundancy and pensions.
+ The Labour Party was established by the trade unions, and some trade unions are affiliated to the Labour Party and give it financial support.
+ Craft groups have existed since the Middle Ages and were called Guilds. With the development of the factory system and industrialisation in the eighteenth century workers began to form what we now would call trade unions. They were associations of people carrying out the same work who acted as a friendly society supporting each other.

Figure 15.2 gives a breakdown of the history of trade unions in the UK.

1799 and 1800	The Combination Acts made virtually all trade union activity illegal and subject to three months' imprisonment.
1834	Trial of 'Tolpuddle Martyrs' from Dorset – agricultural workers who were charged with taking a secret oath to form a trade union and were transported to Australia.
1851	Amalgamated Society of Engineers formed – first of the 'New Model' unions – which had members from a range of industries.
1868	First meeting of the Trades Union Congress (TUC) in Manchester.
1901	Taff Vale judgment makes union funds liable for damages caused by strikes.
1906	Trade Disputes Act reverses Taff Vale judgment.
1926	General strike over wage cuts in mining industry: Royal Commission appointed in response to the defeat of attempts to cut wages. The government responds by calling in troops and volunteers to break the strike. TUC issues order to return to work on 12 May.
1980	Trade union membership peaks at 13 million.
1980–93	Six Employment Acts restrict industrial action by requiring pre-strike ballots, outlawing secondary action, restricting picketing and giving employers the right to seek injunctions where there is doubt about the legality of action.
2021	Trade union membership stands at 6.44 million.

Figure 15.2 The history of trade unions – some important milestones

As Figure 15.2 shows, the history of trade unions in the UK has been one of restrictions being put in place and then later removed as the role of trade unions became more important in society.

In recent years the membership of trade unions has declined, but there is still a very high membership within public services.

> **Tip**
>
> It is not necessary to learn the timeline of the history of the trade unions but only to recognise how they have developed over time. When answering questions on the development of the trade unions you could refer to the Tolpuddle Martyrs and the General Strike of 1926.

Check your understanding and progress at **www.hoddereducation.co.uk/myrevisionnotes**

Employers' associations

Employers' associations are the mirror image of trade unions:

+ They represent the owners of specific sectors of the economy.
+ They seek to influence government; they often negotiate as a body with trade unions regarding pay and conditions.
+ In recent years they were active representing their interests within the EU and many belonged to pan-European employer organisations.

> ### Useful websites
>
> List of all employers' associations in the UK: **www.gov.uk/government/publications/public-list-of-employers-associations-listed-and-unlisted/employers-associations-current-list-and-schedule**
>
> The following are some examples of employer organisations. Some are national bodies, others are regional. They seek to represent the interests of their members.
>
> Association of British Orchestras: **www.abo.org.uk**
>
> British Amusement and Gaming Trades Association: **www.bacta.org.uk**
>
> Federation of Master Builders: **www.fmb.org.uk**
>
> National Farmers Union: **www.nfuonline.com**
>
> Road Haulage Association: **www.rha.uk.net**
>
> University and Colleges Employers Association: **www.ucea.ac.uk**

> ### Case study
>
> **The Federation of Window Cleaners**
>
> The Federation was established in 1947 as an independent, non-profit making organisation to support the needs of window cleaners in the UK. Owned by and run only for the benefit of our members.
>
> Our purpose is to maintain and improve the window cleaning industry and to represent our membership, updating our image in line with the unrivalled federation that we have become today and in turn we continue to re-evaluate the service offering we supply to our membership.
>
> Source: adapted from the Federation of Window Cleaners website: **www.f-w-c.co.uk**.

The nature of criminality in the UK today

REVISED

Differing types of crimes

Government statistics on crime come from two sources:

+ those recorded by the police
+ those recorded in the Crime Survey for England and Wales (CSEW).

The CSEW measures the public's perception of crime. It tends to use broader categories than the police use to record crime (see Figure 15.3).

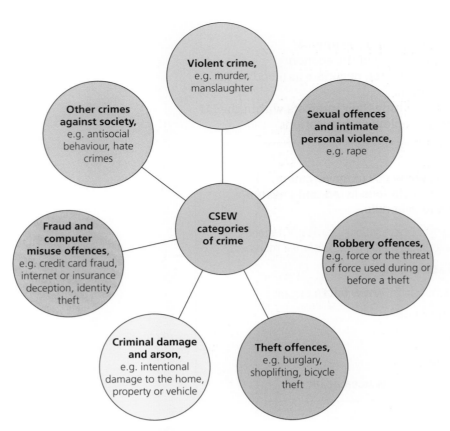

Figure 15.3 CSEW categories of crime

Gathering data on crime

It is important to note that:

+ Recorded crime data cover a wider population and broader set of offences than the CSEW records.
+ The police data do not include any crimes that don't come to their attention.
+ The CSEW figures are based on face-to-face surveys that ask citizens about a range of crimes.
+ The CSEW includes responses from adults and children.
+ The CSEW includes crimes that are not reported to or recorded by the police.

Table 15.2 gives an overview of the main types of crime occurring in England and Wales in April 2022.

Table 15.2 Main types of crime in England and Wales, April 2022

Offence	Number of incidents
Violence	1,789,000
Homicide	691
Knife or sharp instruments	46,950
Theft	2,910,000
Burglary	258,185
Vehicle offences	348,481
Robbery	62,354
Fraud	5,189,000
Computer misuse	1,841,000

Source: Office for National Statistics – Crime Survey for England and Wales (CSEW) and the Telephone-operated Crime Survey for England and Wales (TCSEW), Home Office – Police recorded crime (PRC)

Activity

It is always helpful to research the latest crime data on the ONS website: **www.ons.gov.uk**

Check your understanding and progress at **www.hoddereducation.co.uk/myrevisionnotes**

Profile of criminality in the UK

In 2012, a government-sponsored report entitled 'Prisoners' Childhood and Family Backgrounds' looked at the past and present family circumstances of 1435 newly sentenced (in 2005 and 2006) prisoners. Its key findings were:

+ 24 per cent stated that they had been in care at some point during their childhood
+ 29 per cent of prisoners had experienced abuse and 41 per cent had observed violence in the home as a child.
+ 37 per cent of prisoners reported having family members who had been convicted of a non-motoring criminal offence. Of those prisoners, 84 per cent had a family member who had been in prison, a young offenders' institution or borstal
+ 18 per cent of prisoners stated that they had a family member with an alcohol problem, and 14 per cent had a family member with a drug problem.
+ 59 per cent of prisoners stated that they had regularly played truant from school, 63 per cent had been suspended or temporarily excluded, and 42 per cent stated that they had been permanently excluded or expelled.

The Home Office research paper on youth crime showed that youngsters commit a 'disproportionate' amount of crime, as under-18s make up one-tenth of the population but are responsible for 23 per cent of offences.

Gender and crime

In 2019 females made up 51 per cent of the population, but only accounted for:

+ 15 per cent of arrests
+ 27 per cent of convictions
+ 5 per cent of the prison population.

Age and crime

Figure 15.4 indicates the age of offending – showing that 17 is the peak age for offending.

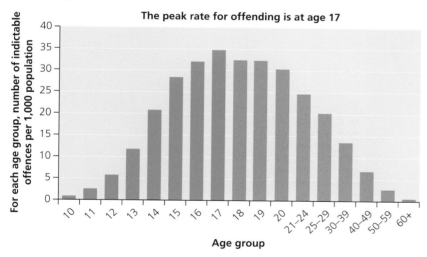

The peak rate for offending is at age 17

Figure y-axis: For each age group, number of indictable offences per 1,000 population

Age group

Figure 15.4 The age of offenders

Factors affecting crime rates in society and strategies to reduce crime

While people have questioned how crime rate statistics are gathered in the UK, especially those by the different local police forces, this element of the course is concerned with societal issues affecting the crime rate. Figure 15.5 takes a closer look at these factors.

Figure 15.5 Factors affecting the crime rate

Figure 15.6 summaries the strategies used to reduce crime in England and Wales.

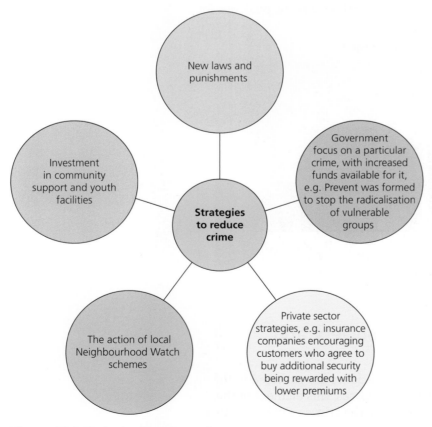

Figure 15.6 Strategies to reduce crime

Check your understanding and progress at **www.hoddereducation.co.uk/myrevisionnotes**

How we deal with those who commit crime

The purposes of sentencing

The Criminal Justice Act 2003 stated that there were five purposes of sentencing:

1 Punishing the offender.
2 Deterrence.
3 Rehabilitation of the offender.
4 Protection for the community.
5 Reparations by the offender.

Differing forms of punishment in the UK

In the criminal justice system in the UK there are two categories of punishment: custodial and non-custodial (see Table 15.3).

Table 15.3 Custodial and non-custodial sentences

Sentence	Commentary
Custodial (imprisonment)	
Prison	Offenders normally serve half their sentence in prison, and the rest on licence in the community.
	If they break the conditions of their licence, they can be sent back to prison.
Life sentence	Must be given to those found guilty of murder.
	The judge sets a minimum term before the parole board can consider release.
Extended sentence	A person can be released on licence for up to eight years.
Determinate sentence	Fixed term in prison. Early release on licence depends upon behaviour.
Suspended sentence	Sentenced up to two years but carries out a court order such as unpaid work, or receives treatment for drugs or alcohol to avoid serving the time in prison.
Non-custodial (not involving imprisonment)	
Community service	Community sentences both: + punish, e.g. through unpaid work removing graffiti + try to help people stay out of trouble, e.g. through treatment for drug addiction.
Fines	Fines are for less severe offences and are the most common type of sentence.
	The fine is set by the court after considering the seriousness of the offence and how much money the offender has.
Ancillary orders	These impose upon the person conditions relating to their behaviour. Examples include: + drink banning order + compensation order + restraining order + football banning order.
Discharge	These are used for the least serious offences for which the experience of being taken to court is thought to be punishment enough. But a discharge can come with conditions that mean the offender must stay out of trouble.

> **Tip**
>
> Remember that the phrase 'punishment' relates to criminal offences; 'damages' are awarded in a civil case.

15 How the law protects the citizen and deals with criminals (3.3.3)

119

The effectiveness of different types of sentences

+ It is difficult to measure the effectiveness of different types of sentences.
+ The main way to measure effectiveness is through reoffending rates.
+ In reoffending rate statistics, reoffending is defined as any new offence committed within a one-year follow-up period that leads to a court conviction, caution, reprimand or warning.
+ According to UK government statistics published in 2022, the overall proven reoffending rate was 24.7 per cent. Since 2017, this rate has fluctuated between 24.7 and 31.8 per cent.
+ The rate is higher for juvenile offenders (34.1 per cent), adults released from custody or starting court orders (31.8 per cent), and adults released from custodial sentences of less than 12 months.

How the youth justice system operates

The youth justice system deals with people aged 10–17. There are three aspects to consider:
+ the Youth Justice Board
+ Youth Offending Teams
+ Youth Courts.

Youth Justice Board

+ The Youth Justice Board (YJB) for England and Wales is a body set up by the government.
+ It works closely with Youth Offending Teams (YOTs).
+ The Board oversees and supports the performance of the youth justice system regarding its main aim, which is to prevent children and young people from offending.
+ The YJB provides national coordination, guidance and monitoring of locally managed YOT partnerships.
+ It is responsible for commissioning secure accommodation for young people who have been sentenced or remanded by the courts.

Youth Offending Teams

+ YOTs are a partnership of organisations (including the police) with a legal responsibility to prevent offending and reduce reoffending.
+ YOTs involve community volunteers in their work and help to develop skills to engage with young people.

Youth Courts

+ When a young person is charged with an offence, they will appear before the Youth Court.
+ If the case cannot be dealt with immediately, the Court will make a decision as to whether the young person will be bailed or remanded into custody.
+ If a young person pleads not guilty, a date will be set for the trial.
+ If the decision is guilty, the magistrates will decide on the most appropriate sentence.
+ If the case is very serious, the Youth Court will send the case to the Crown Court for trial and/or sentence.
+ A Youth Court is made up of three magistrates or a district judge.
+ There is no jury in a Youth Court.
+ A parent or guardian of the accused must attend if the accused is under 16 years old.
+ The Court can give a range of community sentences or detention and training orders, which are served in a secure centre for young people.

Figure 15.7 indicates the informal nature of the Court and identifies those who attend.

A — Witness

B — Magistrates

C — Clerk of the court

D — Lawyers for the prosecution and defence

E — Defendant

F — Parent

G — Youth offending team worker

H — Usher

Figure 15.7 A Youth Court in session

Useful websites

The Howard League for Penal Reform: **www.howardleague.org**

NACRO (National Association for the Care and Resettlement of Offenders): **www. nacro.org.uk**

Office for National Statistics: **www.ons.gov.uk/**

Sentencing Council – the body responsible for reviewing the application of sentences: **www.sentencingcouncil.org.uk/about-sentencing/types-of-sentence/**

Trades Union Congress: **www.tuc.org.uk**

Unite: **www.unitetheunion.org**

Youth Justice Board for England and Wales: **www.gov.uk/government/organisations/ youth-justice-board-for-england-and-wales/about**

Youth Justice statistics for England and Wales (published each year; Ministry of Justice statistics website publishes important youth justice statistics every three months): **www.gov.uk/government/statistics/youth-justice-statistics-2020-to-2021**

Key points check

Can you answer the key points related to this chapter? If you are unclear about how to respond to any of these questions, revisit the relevant topics in the chapter.

+ How have human rights developed and changed?
+ What do we mean by the right to representation?
+ How do we define different crimes?
+ What is the profile of criminality in the UK?
+ What factors affect crime rates?
+ How does society deal with criminality?
+ How are young people treated in the justice system?

Now test yourself (AO1)

1 Identify one of the two types of sentences given out by judges.
2 What is the peak age for offending?
3 Define what is meant by the term 'rehabilitation'.
4 Explain the term 'common law'.
5 Name the national body that has oversight of young people who commit crime.

Exam practice

1 With reference to Figure 15.7 on page 121, compare how the composition and workings of the Youth Court differ from that of a Magistrates' Court. [4] (AO2)

2 Justify the case for increasing the resources given to help those released from prison. [8] (AO3)

3* Analyse why in a democracy parliament needs to pass laws about how trade unions operate.

In your answer you should consider:
+ the role of trade unions
+ how and why parliament has passed laws about trade unions. [8] (AO3)

Remember, the * means this is a synoptic question, which draws upon your knowledge and understanding from more than one theme. You can find more information on page 10.

Check your understanding and progress at **www.hoddereducation.co.uk/myrevisionnotes**

16 Universal human rights (3.3.4)

International human rights agreements and treaties

The Universal Declaration of Human Rights

+ The UN Universal Declaration of Human Rights (UDHR) was published in 1948.
+ It is the key legislation in regard to the recent development of human rights.
+ It is made up of 30 elements.

Figure 16.1 shows some of the key rights enshrined in the Declaration.

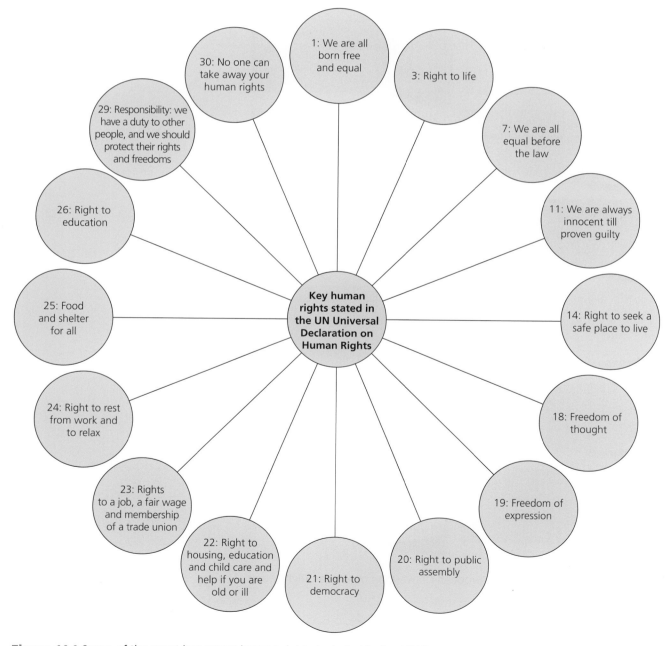

Figure 16.1 Some of the most important human rights included in the UDHR

The European Convention on Human Rights

+ The European Convention on Human Rights and Fundamental Freedoms (ECHR) is an international agreement adopted in 1950, which came into force in September 1953.
+ The Convention and the European Court of Human Rights (ECHR) are part of the structure of the Council of Europe.
+ The Convention ensured the rights stated in the UDHR came into effect in European countries and established an international court with powers to find fault against states that do not fulfil their undertakings.
+ The court sits in Strasbourg, France, and is made up of judges from each of the member countries.
+ The UK was one of the first countries to agree to the ECHR and played a key role in the drafting of the Convention. The Convention has been updated several times since 1953 (see Figure 16.2).

> **Tip**
>
> It is not necessary to know every single article. Try to remember a few to be able to quote to show understanding of the extent of the Charter. Bear in mind that this Declaration was drafted in 1948, so in some areas of human rights it can appear dated. For more details, see **www.un.org/en/our-work/protect-human-rights**.

Article 1: Obligation to respect human rights	Article 8: Right to respect for private and family life, home and correspondence
Article 2: Right to life	Article 9: Freedom of thought, conscience and religion
Article 3: Prohibition of torture, inhuman and degrading treatment	Article 10: Freedom of expression
Article 4: Prohibition of slavery and forced labour	Article 11: Freedom of assembly and association
Article 5: Right to liberty and security	Article 12: Right to marry
Article 6: Right to a fair trial	Article 13: Right to an effective remedy
Article 7: No punishment without law	Article 14: Prohibition of discrimination

Figure 16.2 The Articles of the European Convention on Human Rights

Check your understanding and progress at **www.hoddereducation.co.uk/myrevisionnotes**

The UN Convention on the Rights of the Child

✚ The UN Convention on the Rights of the Child (UNCRC) was signed in September 1990 and all members of the UN, with the exception of the USA, have ratified it.
✚ In total there are 54 articles in the UNCRC.
✚ It was incorporated into UK law in 1992.

Figure 16.3 illustrates the duties the UNCRC places on governments in regard to the rights of children.

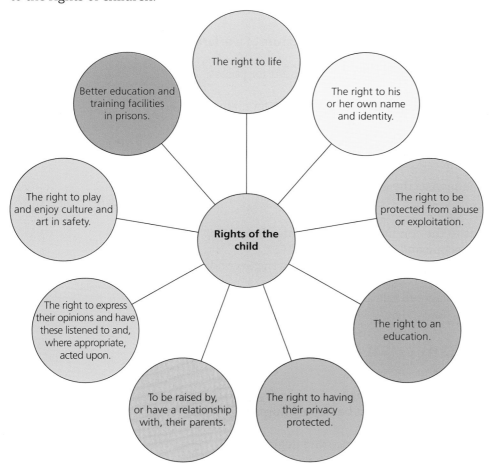

Figure 16.3 UN Convention on the Rights of the Child

The Human Rights Act 1998 (UK legislation)

✚ The Human Rights Act (HRA) 1998 ensured that the European Convention on Human Rights was embedded in UK law.
✚ This meant that UK citizens could bring cases before UK courts and have them resolved without having to go to the court in Strasbourg.

+ It also meant that UK courts had to abide by and take account of decisions of the court in Strasbourg when arriving at their own decisions.
+ It also stated that UK public bodies had to abide by the European Convention.

The role of international law in conflict situations

How international humanitarian law helps establish the rules of war

International humanitarian law (IHL) aims to:
+ protect people who are not involved or are no longer involved in hostilities, for example, the sick and wounded, prisoners and civilians
+ set out the rights and obligations of those involved in the armed conflict.

Two important conventions that led to the development of the concept of international humanitarian law are the Geneva Conventions and the Hague Convention, which set out to protect the victims of war.

The Geneva Convention
+ The Geneva Convention was established after the Battle of Solferino in 1864 to help those involved and wounded in the battle.
+ Over the years the Convention has been extended as the nature of warfare has changed, particularly in its impact upon civilians.
    + The Convention was extended in 1906 and 1929 (to account for poison gas).
    + In 1949 its scope was extended again, to include protection for civilians following the events of the Second World War.
    + It was further extended in 1977 and 2005 to account for landmines and biological weapons and to ensure the protection of children in armed conflicts.
+ The International Red Cross is seen as the guardian of the Convention.

The Hague Convention
+ The Hague Convention relates to the conduct of war and dates from 1899. Over time it has broadened its scope and was amended in 1907.
+ It was used as a basis for the Nuremberg war trials following the Second World War.
+ In 1980, a Hague Convention was agreed relating to child trafficking and abduction.

How international humanitarian law protects civilians during conflicts

International humanitarian law states the following:
+ Civilians under the power of enemy forces must be treated humanely in all circumstances.
+ They must be protected against all forms of violence and degrading treatment, including murder and torture. If arrested they are entitled to a fair trial.
+ Those trying to help them – medical units, humanitarian or relief bodies providing essentials such as food, clothing and medical supplies – should be given protection and access to help.
+ Priority should be given to women and children, the aged and sick, who are highly vulnerable during armed conflicts. So too are those who flee their homes and become internally displaced or refugees. International humanitarian law prohibits forced movement by intimidation, violence or starvation.

+ Families are often separated in armed conflict. States must take all appropriate steps to prevent this and take action to re-establish family contact by providing information and facilitating tracing activities.

International Criminal Court

+ At the end of the Second World War, the Allies set up the Nuremberg and Tokyo war trials, through which individuals and organisations were charged with war crimes, crimes against peace and crimes against humanity.
+ In the 1990s, international criminal tribunals for the former Yugoslavia and for Rwanda were set up by international agreement to deal with war crimes that took place in the two regions.
+ In 1998, 120 countries signed the Rome Statute, which established a permanent International Criminal Court (ICC).
+ The court sits at The Hague in The Netherlands.
+ The ICC has opened a number of investigations regarding alleged abuses in the Democratic Republic of the Congo, the Central African Republic, Uganda, Sudan, Kenya and Libya.
+ The treaty establishing the Court defined what is meant by 'war crimes' as wilful killing, torture, wilful causing great suffering, extensive destruction of property, forcing prisoners of war to serve in hostile forces, not offering POWs a right to a trial, unlawful deportation and taking hostages.

Useful websites

Amnesty International: **www.amnesty.org.uk/**

British Institute of Human Rights: **www.bihr.org.uk**

Equality and Human Rights Commission: **www.equalityhumanrights.com**

European Court of Human Rights: **www.echr.coe.int**

Geneva Convention: **www.icrc.org/en/war-and-law/treaties-customary-law/geneva-conventions**

Human Rights Investigations: **http://humanrightsinvestigations.org**

International Criminal Court: **www.icc-cpi.int**

International Committee of the Red Cross: **www.icrc.org**

Liberty: **www.libertyhumanrights.org.uk/**

Office of the United Nations High Commissioner for Human Rights (OHCHR): **www.ohchr.org/en/ohchr_homepage**

UK Children's Commissioners to protect and enforce the rights of children: **www.childrenscommissioner.gov.uk**

UNICEF: **www.unicef.org**

United Nations: **www.un.org/en/our-work/protect-human-rights**

Key points check

Can you answer the key points related to this chapter? If you are unclear about how to respond to any of these questions, revisit the relevant topics in the chapter.
+ Why are the UDHR and the ECHR important?
+ What are the Rights of the Child?
+ Why is the Human Rights Act 1998 important?
+ Why is international law important?

Now test yourself (AO1)

TESTED

1 Which Convention is the responsibility of the Council of Europe?
2 Identify an aim of international humanitarian law.
3 Identify two reasons why the UDHR is important.
4 Name the Convention that the Human Rights Act incorporated into UK law in 1998.
5 Name the organisation that oversees the operation of the Geneva Convention.

Source A: human rights abuses in Syria

> During recent years the civil war in Syria has led to many people being forced out of their homes and seeking refuge in other countries. Both sides have killed many non-combatants and the Syrian government has been accused of using chemical weapons on its fellow citizens.

1 Consider the ways in which international humanitarian law seeks to protect the non-combatants described in Source A. [4] (AO2)

2 The United Nations Declaration of Human Rights was agreed in 1948, more than 70 years ago. Present a case to justify changes you would make to its content to make it fit for the next 70 years. [8] (AO3)

3* Justify the arguments put forward by those UK politicians who wish the UK to withdraw from the European Convention on Human Rights.

   In your answer you should consider:
   + the content of the European Convention on Human Rights and how it operates
   + the reasons some UK politicians are unhappy with the way the Convention operates. [8] (AO3)

Remember, the * means this is a synoptic question, which draws upon your knowledge and understanding from more than one theme. You can find more information on page 10.

Check your understanding and progress at **www.hoddereducation.co.uk/myrevisionnotes**

Glossary

Term	Definition	Page/s
Advocacy	Speaking out to promote a cause or an issue.	13
Apathy	A lack of interest by citizens in the electoral and political process.	11
Backbencher	A member of the House of Commons who is not a government minister or opposition spokesperson. They sit behind the front row of seats in the chamber, hence the name backbencher.	63
Barrister	Graduates who become specialists in a narrow aspect of the law and are employed by solicitors on behalf of their clients to represent them.	106
Bicameral	The name given to a parliament made up of two chambers, like the UK system with the House of Commons and the House of Lords.	58
Boycott	Refusing to buy goods or use a service in order to achieve a desired political outcome. The original term related to Captain Boycott, an Irish landowner whose tenants refused to pay their rent.	96
Brexit	A slogan used by the Leave campaign in the 2016 EU referendum to signify its aims. The 'Br' stood for Britain or the UK, and 'exit' for leaving the European Union.	25
British values	The values that are associated with living in modern-day Britain.	72
Budget	An annual statement made by the chancellor of the exchequer to the House of Commons about the taxation policy for the forthcoming year.	19
By-election	An election held in a seat after the retirement or death of the sitting member.	55
Central government	Term used to describe the government of the United Kingdom.	15
Chief constable	The chief police officer within each regional police force.	19
Citizens Advice office	Locally based offices of Citizens Advice, a registered charity that provides advice, support and help related to a range of issues including legal, financial and consumer, and issues relating to local authorities and central government services.	28
Citizenship	A legal status conferred by a state upon members of the state, indicating their membership of the state.	29
Civil law	The type of law that deals with disputes between individuals when damages are awarded.	88
Civil service	Employees of the state who administer public policy.	39
Coalition government	A government formed by more than one party. The parties agree on a policy platform and each holds posts within the government. These arrangements can be for a fixed term or for a full parliament, as in 2010.	57
Common law	Law based upon judges' rulings in court.	105
Commonwealth Charter	A document that lays down the principles associated with Commonwealth membership.	95
Communism	A classless system where there is no private property, the means of production are collectively owned, and the only political party is the Communist Party, e.g. Russia (until 1991) and China.	59
Conservatism	An eighteenth-century political ideology based upon a traditional belief in the family, the Church and nationalism. It has a paternalistic approach to community affairs. This ideology has evolved to encompass parties from the New Right to the Christian Democrats.	59
Constituency	A named geographical area consisting on average of between 56,000 voters in Wales and 72,200 in England, who elect a single MP to the UK Parliament. All parliamentary boundaries are currently being reviewed and will be finalised in July 2023, with the aim that all constituencies (with the exception of those composed of islands) will consist of around 73,000 electors.	46
Council of Europe	Was founded in 1949 and is an intergovernmental organisation that aims to promote human rights, democracy and the rule of law within its 47 member states. This body established the European Convention on Human Rights.	91

My Revision Notes: AQA GCSE (9–1) Citizenship Studies

Council of the European Union	Meetings of ministers from member states of the EU.	92
Councillor	A citizen who is elected to serve on local councils.	11
Criminal law	The type of law where individuals are charged by the state with an offence and if found guilty are punished by the state.	110
Crown Prosecution Service (CPS)	An independent government body that determines whether charges should be brought. It prosecutes cases in the courts on behalf of the state.	18
Custodial	A sentence that involves imprisonment.	55
Democracy	A political system based upon the concept of people having the power to decide through an open and fair electoral system, where electors can choose from competing political parties or groups. The word comes from the ancient Greek for people and power.	11
Deterrence	A principle associated with sentencing policy. It aims to reduce levels of crime as a result of those considering a criminal act not carrying out that act due to the nature of the sentence they will receive.	119
Devolution	The transfer of power from a greater body to a lesser body, e.g. the UK Parliament granting powers to Scotland.	36
Devolved and reserved powers	Devolved powers are those transferred by the UK government to the devolved governments. Reserved powers are those that are still held by the UK government.	45
Devolved government	Name given to the bodies created under the policy of devolution, e.g. the Scottish Parliament.	44
Direct democracy	A system of government where all citizens take part in decision-making. A modern form of direct democracy is the use of referendums.	35
Directly elected mayors	Posts within local councils in England and Wales that are directly elected by the voters. They are responsible for the running and direction of their local council. It is one of several ways in which local councils can be organised. One of the first to be created was the Mayor of London.	36
Discrimination	Treating a person or group of people unfairly on the basis of their sex, gender, race, etc.	27
Electoral Commission	A government-established body that monitors and oversees all UK elections and referendums.	49
Emigration	When people leave their own country to live permanently elsewhere.	80
E-petition	A way citizens can request parliament to debate an issue. If a petition attracts 100,000 signatures, a committee of MPs decides whether it is suitable for debate in parliament.	14
Equality	The concept that everyone should have an equal opportunity to make the most of their life and talents.	27
Equality Act 2010	Brought together 116 pieces of legislation to provide Britain with a new discrimination law to protect individuals from unfair treatment. Promotes a fair and more equal society.	37
Equality and Human Rights Commission	Established in 2007, it took over the work of three previous equality organisations: the Commission for Racial Equality (CRE), the Disability Rights Commission (DRC) and the Equal Opportunities Commission (EOC), as well as taking on responsibility for protecting and promoting equality and human rights for everyone. It is a statutory non-departmental government body.	27
Euro	The common currency used by the Eurozone.	93
European Commission	Appointed officials from member countries of the EU who draft policy initiatives and direct the workings of the EU.	92
European Convention on Human Rights	A convention that lays down basic human rights. It is based upon the UDHR and is overseen by the Council of Europe.	94
European Council	Meetings of the heads of government of EU member states.	92
European Court of Human Rights (ECHR)	Court of the Council of Europe that sits in Strasbourg and rules on the European Convention on Human Rights. It must not be confused with the European Court of Justice, which is the court of the European Union.	94

Check your understanding and progress at **www.hoddereducation.co.uk/myrevisionnotes**

European Parliament	The directly elected parliament of the European Union.	47
Executive	An element of government made up of government ministers, advisers and senior civil servants who determine the policy of government.	57
Fairness	Treating people equally and according to the circumstances.	99
Freedom	The ability to act, speak or think as one likes.	13
Frontbencher	A government minister or shadow minister who sits on the front row of seats in the House of Commons chamber. The two groups face each other across the table in the chamber.	62
G7	A forum for the leaders of the seven richest countries in the world to meet and discuss economic and political issues. Its members are Canada, France, Germany, Italy, Japan, the United Kingdom and the United States. The EU President of the Commission also attends.	97
General election	An election when the entire UK Parliament is elected. Under the Fixed-term Parliaments Act 2011, elections were held after a fixed five-year period from the previous election, but this Act was repealed in 2020.	12
Geneva Conventions	The most important conventions relating to how civilians and others should be treated during a time of war.	126
Gross domestic product (GDP)	The value of all the goods and services created in a country, normally measured on an annual basis.	51
Gross national income (GNI)	GDP minus income earned by non-residents plus income received from non-residents.	97
Group identity	The identity associated with belonging to a group.	82
Hague Convention	Deals with the rules governing the conduct of war.	126
House of Commons	The first chamber of parliament, made up of 650 elected members. The government is formed based on the composition of this chamber. It is a legislative chamber that also holds the government to account.	25
House of Lords	The second chamber of parliament. Since 1911, it is far less important than the House of Commons. Its main purpose is as a revising chamber. Made up of non-elected members.	36
Humanitarian aid	Non-military aid given to countries and people in need, for example food, shelter, medical help.	95
Human right	A fundamental right that every person is entitled to have, to be or to do.	20
Human Rights Act (HRA)	Passed in 1998 and came into force in 2000. This Act brought together numerous pieces of human rights legislation and gave UK citizens easier access to the European Court of Human Rights.	94
Identity	The characteristics that determine whom or what a person is.	74
Immigration	The movement of people who come to live permanently in a foreign country. For example people from Hong Kong moving to live permanently in the UK.	79
IMPRESS	The official press regulator.	89
Independent Press Standards Organisation (IPSO)	Set up to handle complaints and conduct investigations into standards and compliance.	89
Individual liberty	The concept that in a modern democracy people have the freedom to make their own choices and decisions.	59
Inflation	A rise in the average level of prices over a set period of time, which also corresponds to a fall in the purchasing power of your income.	53
International Criminal Court (ICC)	Set up in 1998 to try persons indicted for crimes against humanity or war crimes. By 2020, 120 nations had agreed to work with the Court.	127
International humanitarian law (IHL)	A body of law associated with international disputes and the conduct of war and people affected by war.	126
Judiciary	The part of the UK system of governance that is responsible for its legal system and that consists of all the judges in its courts of law.	35

My Revision Notes: AQA GCSE (9–1) Citizenship Studies

Jury service	Citizens are required to serve on juries as a civic duty. Twelve people serve in England, Wales and Northern Ireland, 15 in Scotland. They are selected at random from the register of voters.	18
Justice	Behaviour or treatment that is morally right and fair.	18
Lay member	A person who serves on a body/organisation but is not a qualified professional within the specialism of that body. They are there to represent the wider general public.	19
Legal executive	Legally qualified specialists employed largely by solicitors.	107
Legislation	Or statute law; laws passed by parliament.	11
Liberal democracy	A system of government based upon representative democracy and linked to freedoms and rights for citizens.	23
Liberalism	A political philosophy dating from the eighteenth century, based on individual liberty, freedom of worship and free trade. It evolved into social liberalism, with a concern for welfare rights. It encompasses Liberal, Free Democratic and Radical parties.	59
Local election	Elections held for councillors to local councils, held on a fixed date in May after the fixed term of office has expired.	35
Lord Speaker	The Speaker of the House of Lords.	62
Lords Spiritual	The 26 bishops of the Church of England who are members of the House of Lords.	46
Magistrate	Part-time community volunteers who determine verdicts and sentences in local Magistrates' Courts.	18
Magna Carta	Known as the Great Charter, signed by King John in 1215. It established the rights and powers of the king and the people of England.	35
Manifesto	A document produced by a political party at the time of an election, outlining the policies it would like to introduce.	51
Mass media	The means of communicating to a large number of people at the same time, e.g. television, newspapers, the internet, social media.	85
Mediation	A process of involving outsiders in a dialogue to try to resolve a dispute between two parties.	95
Member of Parliament (MP)	A citizen elected to parliament who serves in parliament, normally as a member of a political party.	24
Migration	The movement of people out of one country and into another.	72
Multiculturalism	A concept regarding the co-existence of diverse cultures in a society. A multicultural society is one in which these different groups live side by side and there is a mutual respect for each group's culture and traditions.	72
Multicultural society	A society that comprises people from a range of cultural, ethnic and religious backgrounds.	81
Multiple identity	The concept that a person can assume different identities at different times and in different situations.	82
National identity	An identity associated with being a citizen of a specific country.	75
Nature v. nurture	A debate about whether a person's personality and identity are most affected by their biological background or by the way in which they are brought up.	82
Neighbourhood Watch	A voluntary scheme in which people in a given area work with the police to help reduce crime.	19
Net migration	The difference in the number of people coming to live in a country and the number who leave a country to live in another country.	80
New media	All non-traditional forms of media.	85
New Right	A view of conservatism linked to Margaret Thatcher and the Conservative Party in the UK and Ronald Reagan and the Republican Party in the USA. The New Right ideology argued for less state provision, less state interference in business and lower taxation, in order to increase national wealth and allow for greater personal empowerment and social mobility.	59
Non-custodial	A criminal sentence that does not involve imprisonment.	108
Non-democratic	A system of government that lacks some or all of the elements that make up a democratic political system.	69

Check your understanding and progress at **www.hoddereducation.co.uk/myrevisionnotes**

Non-departmental public body (NDPB)	A body that has a role in the processes of government but is not part of government. Formerly a quango. *See Quango.*	65
Non-governmental organisation (NGO)	Can be national or international. Many of them are charities that provide services to those in need, similar to those provided by government. Many work with government agencies and can receive funds from government.	97
Ofcom	The Office of Communications: a government regulator for elements of the media industry.	89
Office for National Statistics (ONS)	A government body that collects and provides background data.	75
Police and crime commissioner	A directly elected official who is responsible for the running of a regional police force outside London.	11
Pressure group	An organised body of citizens who share a common interest in an issue and promote their cause through a variety of actions.	12
The prime minister	The head of government in the UK; the monarch is head of state. In the USA, the president holds both posts. The prime minister is normally the leader of the largest party in the House of Commons and is an MP. They are appointed by the monarch after a general election and have the title First Lord of the Treasury.	35
Prime Minister's Questions (PMQs)	30 minutes each Wednesday when the prime minister faces questions from MPs in the chamber of the House of Commons. Six questions are allocated to the leader of the opposition.	61
Principle	A basic truth or idea that underpins a system of beliefs associated with a given society.	34
Private Members' Bill (PMB)	A bill, a draft for a law, that is proposed by an MP. A lottery is held each year and if an MP comes out towards the top, they stand a chance of their bill becoming law.	62
Proportional representation	A system of voting whereby the number of people elected relates to the number (percentage) of votes cast.	35
Proxy	In regard to voting, allowing another to vote on your behalf. You have to officially apply and nominate a named person to be your proxy.	55
Quango	A quasi-autonomous non-governmental organisation. These are bodies that work with government, sometimes carrying out services on behalf of government and funded by government, but partially independent from government. Government now uses the term 'NDPBs' to describe them, as the word 'quango' has become associated with negative media coverage of these bodies.	65
Recorded crime	Crimes that are reported to and recorded by the police.	116
Referendum	A vote on a single issue, where governments or other bodies wish to seek the views of electors on an issue, for example the 2016 referendum on the UK's membership of the European Union.	12
Rehabilitation	An aim of sentencing, seeking to change the behaviour of the offender.	119
Reparation	Where an offender has to pay towards the damage they have caused.	119
Representative democracy	A system of government where citizens are elected to represent others in an assembly. A UK example of such a citizen would be an MP or councillor.	23
Reserved powers	Powers still held by the UK Parliament on behalf of all parts of the UK, e.g. constitutional affairs, defence and foreign policy.	45
Responsibility	The state or fact of having to do something.	11
Right	A moral or legal entitlement to have or do something.	11
Rule of law	A basic principle of a democratic society that the law applies equally to all people.	72
Sanctions	Measures taken by a state against others to achieve a change in policy or action.	95
Secondary action	When a worker not directly involved in a trade dispute takes action to support other workers.	114
Security Council	The major decision-making body of the United Nations. Made up of five permanent members and ten elected member countries. The UK is one of the permanent members.	91
Socialism	A political ideology dating mainly from the nineteenth century, based upon the common ownership of the economy, equality and opportunity. It encompasses parties ranging from Communists to Social Democrats.	59

133

My Revision Notes: AQA GCSE (9–1) Citizenship Studies

Social media	The ways in which people interact with each other on the internet, for example Twitter and Facebook.	11
Soft power	The ability to influence others through the influence of your culture, as well as through your political and foreign policy values.	91
Solicitor	Mainly law graduates who cover a range of legal work, both civil and criminal, and have to be formally qualified.	106
Sovereignty	The power and authority that a country has to make decisions about itself and its relations with others.	37
The Speaker	A Member of Parliament elected by other members to chair the proceedings of the House of Commons and manage the business of the House.	25
Special adviser	Specialist and political advisers to ministers and opposition spokespersons; they can have temporary civil service status, paid for by the taxpayer.	65
Special constable	Volunteers who help the police on a part-time basis in their local community. They have the same powers as a regular police constable, though are unpaid.	19
Strike	The withdrawal of one's labour; refusing to work.	114
Supplementary vote (SV)	A voting system used in the UK where voters have a second vote that is used in the election process if no candidate gets 50 per cent of the first-choice votes.	57
Supreme Court	The final court of appeal in the UK for civil cases, and for criminal cases from England, Wales and Northern Ireland. It hears cases of great public or constitutional importance that affect the whole population.	35
Tiers	Another term for levels of government.	41
Tolerance	A concept based upon the idea that in a modern society people show understanding of others with differing views and opinions.	59
Trades Union Congress (TUC)	A national body representing most trade unions in the UK.	20
Trade union	An organisation that employees join to provide collective representation with employers regarding, for example, pay, conditions of employment, and health and safety issues. An example would be the National Union of Rail, Maritime and Transport Workers (RMT), which represents those working on the London Underground.	12
Traditional media	Newsprint, radio, television, cinema.	85
Transnational group	A political grouping in the European Parliament made up of MEPs from several countries.	68
Two-party system	A political system that is dominated by two political parties, each of which may at some time form a government.	59
Ultra vires	Acting beyond your legal power or authority.	41
United Nations Charter	A document that lays down the aims of the United Nations.	91
Universal Declaration of Human Rights (UDHR)	An international law setting out a set of universal human rights under the auspices of the United Nations.	72
Values	Standards of behaviour that are accepted by a society.	35
Veto	The ability to vote down any decision.	91
Volunteering	Giving your time without pay to help others.	14
Voter turnout	The number of voters who actually vote, against the total number who could vote, normally expressed as a percentage.	35
Whips	Members of Parliament appointed by their party leader to organise their MPs, ensuring their attendance and their vote.	62

Check your understanding and progress at **www.hoddereducation.co.uk/myrevisionnotes**